OUTRAGE AT LINCHENG

OUTRAGE AT LINCHENG

China Enters the Twentieth Century

Michael J. Nozinski

Glenbridge Publishing Ltd.

"A Week-End with Chinese Bandits," by Lucy Truman Aldrich, first appeared in *The Atlantic Monthly*, November 1923 and is reprinted with permission.

Copyright © 1990 by Michael J. Nozinski

All rights reserved. Except for brief quotations in critical articles or reviews, this book or parts thereof, must not be reproduced in any form without permission in writing from the publisher. For further information contact Glenbridge Publishing Ltd., Macomb, Illinois 61455

Library of Congress Catalog Card Number: 89-80780

International Standard Book Number: 0-944435-07-6

Printed in the U.S.A.

for

David M. Nozinski

CONTENTS

List of Illustrations ix
Foreword xiii
Acknowledgments xix
The Major Players xxi

I.	The Attack 1
II.	Hostage 14
III.	Foreign Meddling 20
IV.	"It's Musso and I think he's dead!" 35
V.	"The bandits looked and behaved like soldiers" ... 46
VI.	Climb to the Summit 57
VII.	Negotiations 69
VIII.	Early Naval Barbarians 81
IX.	Haggling over the Loot? 105
X.	"They use our towels, glasses, cups. . ." 120
XI.	International Pressure 144
XII.	Lincheng Committee 168

Appendix 187
Notes 213
Select Bibliography 231
General Bibliography 235
Index 241

ILLUSTRATIONS

Following p. 13

1. Wreckage of baggage car and first class coach of the Tientsin-Pukow Blue Express

2. Chinese workmen clearing away wreckage

3. Shortly after the attack

4. An evening of poker

5. Inside the dining car

6. The passengers dined on a varied cuisine

7. Luxurious chairs and stained glass

8. Sleeping car

9. End of car

Following p. 68

10. Scenic Mt. Pao Tzu Ku

11. Jerome Henley "on parole" at the mines

12. Marcel Berube

13. The bandit "secretary" Kuo Chi-tsai

14. Major Roland Pinger near the entrance of the "Sap Club"

15. At the Temple stronghold

16. Roy Anderson

17. Lee Solomon and J. B. Powell

18. Cartoon— "People's Self-Deliverance Army"

                Following p. 119

19. The Temples Among the Clouds

20. The Siege

21. Supply train leaving the colliery

22. Cartoon—"The Real Red Peril"

23. Cartoon—"The Child That Never Grew Up"

24. Fred Elias

25. Lee Solomon

                Following p. 143

26. Cartoon—"The monkey bandit dangles out of reach"

27. J. B. Powell, Commodore Musso, and Lee Solomon

28. Group after being ransomed

29. Commodore Musso, J. B. Powell, and Lee Solomon

30. End of train showing metalwork

31. Stamp designed by Carl Crow

32. Journalist J. B. Powell

33. Cartoon—"An educated Chinese bandit in a new military uniform"

Following p. 167

34. Tientsin-Pukow engine

35. Relief car

36. John K. Davis

37. Sleeping compartments and the Drawing Room

38. Private car

Foreword

The Chinese Revolution of 1911 was the culmination of a long struggle in search of modern political, economic, and social institutions that began with China's confrontation with the west in the Opium Wars of 1839–1842. The Revolution of 1911 failed as those who wielded real power knew little about nor had any genuine sympathy for the democratic forms of government. As an ally of the western powers in World War One, China was cast into the maelstrom of international politics and became a victim of the competing rivalries of the several powers.

The Great War resulted in various factions in China aligning themselves with foreign economic interests and thus allowing the warlords, vestiges of the earlier post-Taiping Rebellion era, to become increasingly powerful within their satrapies. The postwar 1920s were, perhaps, the most chaotic years in modern Chinese history. Harsh competition among the imperialist rivals; alliances among corrupt, mostly ill-educated and self-styled military leaders; the breakdown of the long-standing Confucian social order; the disorder of several proclaimed central governments; attempts at national unification by Sun Yat-sen and his supporters, and the emergence of China's own Communist Party armed with an entirely new vision of the future, all made for an era remembered for its corruption and violence.

Chronic civil wars, small-scale though they may have been, kept the society on the brink of economic ruin and spelled poverty and suffering for the masses of peasants and poorly compensated urban workers. The *tuchuns,* or warlords, were local military commanders who often lost favor with the faction in control of the government in Peking and thus found themselves without official support. The warlords were sometimes personally corrupt and failed to pay their troops who then, under the influence of a leader, deserted with their weapons and turned to brigandry. The post-war period also saw attempts to disband the large number of men under arms in China— sometimes without concern for how the soldiers would support themselves. There were also local bandits, rustics whose harsh life had turned them toward violence. In some areas the distinction between these various groups became blurred as they alternately fought and collaborated.

The derailing of the Blue Express presents a dramatic example of the problems that foreign governments faced in trying to protect the lives and property of their nationals in China. Ironically, while the Chinese Revolution was intended to assert China's nationalism and sovereignty against the rapacious policies of the western powers, the political and military conditions in China during the 1920s militated against the relaxation of foreign control. Since the years of the

Opium Wars the western powers seized every pretext to assert greater control over China, and thus its economic potential. A number of western "concessions" were enshrined in a series of agreements, which the Chinese called the "unequal treaties."

Leading the western nations for almost a century were the British who had the largest share of the Chinese concessions and markets. The United States had quietly yielded to British leadership in setting the tone in China, but the postwar decade brought a reassessment by Washington.

Jacob Gould Schurman retired as president of Cornell University in 1920 after twenty-eight years of successful leadership. He had served as President of the First Philippine Commission in 1899 when President William McKinley chose him from among many who voiced criticism of America's mayhem in the islands. The former college president brought to China a genuine concern for China's national interests, a desire to improve the life of her people, and a strong sense of constitutional government and justice. During his years in China he became increasingly concerned with the reluctance of the powers to acknowledge Chinese nationalism and sovereignty.

When the Blue Express was attacked, Schurman detoured to Shantung to go to the site where he played a key role in organizing the relief effort that provided some comfort and assurance to the victims. Schurman also pressed the Chinese Government to take active measures to secure the release of the hostages. He insisted that the Chinese Government accept responsibility for ensuring the safety of the hostages and bringing its wayward militarists under control.

At the same time he resisted the suggestions of those who wished to resolve the problem with foreign troops. More significant, perhaps, was the role the American Minister played in toning down the demands of some of the powers, particularly Great Britain, and preventing the incident from becoming a pretext for the aggressive schemes of the railway police. The late Dr. V. K. Wellington Koo informed me that Minister Schurman did much to mitigate the harshness of the powers' demands over the Lincheng incident and that Koo considered Schurman an ally during those difficult discussions.

The "warlord era" would continue for nearly another decade despite the attempted unification under the nationalist flag of the Kuomintang in 1928. Violence against foreigners increased in the years after the Lincheng incident, and the warlords of China remained treacherous to each other and to outsiders.

Michael Nozinski has painstakingly researched the English language sources in his study of the Lincheng incident. He weaves together the threads of the lives and events of that harrowing month in the mountains of Shantung province. While historians have examined this event from the perspective of warlordism, Chinese politics, imperialism, and international diplomacy, Mr. Nozinski assembles the record from the perspective of the story-teller; he takes us into the filthy way-stations en route to the bandits' lair; he gives us a feeling for the uncertainty and courage that marked the hostages' hours; we are given a peek into the precarious lives of the Chinese bandits, ignorant men for whom shouldering a rifle offered a better life than they had known before, and the ruthless and unscrupulous men who rose to leadership among them. Nozinski leads us into a China that fortunately few have ever come to know.

Dr. Richard C. DeAngelis
Associate Professor of Asian History,
Fairfield University,
Fairfield, Connecticut

Acknowledgments

Librarians and archivists seem a self-selected breed of dedicated and articulate individuals. Without the kind help of the staffs of the following institutions, this book could not have been possible: Rice University; The University of Houston; Texas Southern University; The University of Texas–Austin; The Houston, Vancouver and Victoria Public Libraries; The University of British Columbia; Simon Fraser University; The University of Victoria; The Library of Parliament–Victoria; The United States National Archives; The British Public Record Office.

Permission to use photos or quote copyrighted material is gratefully acknowledged to the following:

"A Week-End With Chinese Bandits," © 1923 by Lucy T. Aldrich, as first published in *The Atlantic Monthly,* November 1923.

The American Car & Foundry for the photos of the Blue Express.

AlCo Historic Photos for the photo of the 4-6-2 light Pacific.

The Illustrated London News Picture Library for the photos printed here by permission.

The Joint Collection, University of Missouri Western Historical Manuscript Collection—Columbia and State Society of Missouri Manuscripts for the photos printed here by permission.

UPI/Bettmann Newsphotos.

My thanks to Dr. Richard C. DeAngelis for material from his excellent study *Jacob Gould Schurman and American Policy Toward China, 1921-1925*, University Microfilms; to Tim Boltbee for his photographic skills; to Ricardo Guerrero Jr. for redrawing the several maps and cartoons; to Ronald D. Eames and Harry A. Fry of the Boston & Maine Railroad Historical Society for their valuable assistance. I thank my parents and family for their kind encouragement, and finally I am eternally grateful to Lin Yu-tang and Lao Tzu.

The Major Players

Lucy Aldrich—a dauntless lady, daughter of Senator Nelson Aldrich and sister-in-law to John D. Rockefeller, Jr.

Major Robert Allen—United States Army Medical Corps, Allen was captured while on leave with his family.

Roy Anderson—born in China of missionary parents, Anderson distinguished himself during the complex negotiations.

Marcel Berube—a Frenchman employed by the Salt monopoly, Burube served as one of the captive messengers to the outside world.

Edna Lee Booker—an intrepid journalist, Booker was the only foreign woman to visit the mines.

Chang Chin-yao—a discredited warlord. Many of the bandits had served in his army.

General William Conner—commander of the United States troops in China.

Alba Coralti—Commodore Musso's editor and secretary, she escaped during the torrential downpour.

Carl Crow—businessman and author, Crow helped to organize the humanitarian relief.

John K. Davis—the United States Consul at Nanking, Davis was the highest ranking American at the colliery rescue site.

J. Bathalha De Freitas—Portugal's Ambassador to China and the "Dean" of Peking's diplomatic corps.

Leon Friedman—an auto dealer from Shanghai, he was held captive to the end.

General Ho Feng-yu—the truculent boss of the coal mines.

Charles Evans Hughes—United States Secretary of State.

Dr. V. K. Wellington Koo—Foreign minister designate, Koo handled the diplomacy on behalf of the Chinese Government.

Kuo Chi-tsai—the bandit "secretary" and second in command.

Lloyd Lehrbas—a reporter for the newspaper *The China Press*, Lehrbas escaped but immediately made his way to the coal mines to cover the story.

Father William Lenfers—a German missionary, Lenfers made several trips into the bandit stronghold.

Li Yuan-hung—President of the Republic of China.

Sir Ronald Macleay—Great Britain's ambassador to China.

Dr. Paul Mertons—a Shanghai physician who repeatedly visited the bandit camps to doctor the foreign captives.

Guiseppe Musso—a wealthy and influential Italian lawyer, he was perhaps the most "valuable" hostage.

Wallace Philoon—United States Assistant Military Attaché.

The Major Players xxiii

John B. Powell—a journalist and the publisher of the *China Weekly Review,* Powell was captured while en route to meet with Dr. Schurman.

Dr. Jacob Gould Schurman—United States Ambassador to China, Schurman played a leading role in the diplomatic maneuvering.

William Smith—"the Manchester Sexagenarian," the irrepressible Smith never let his fellow captives' morale sag too low.

Sun Mei-yao—the leader of the bandits and the man who planned the wrecking of the train.

Sun Yat-sen—physician, revolutionary and statesman, Dr. Sun used the Lincheng outrage to attack the utterly corrupt Peking Government.

Tien Chung-yu—Governor of Shantung province, later dismissed for incompetence.

Tsao Kun—"Inspector General" of Chihli, Shantung, and Honan provinces, and the power behind the throne. Tsao Kun later "purchased" the Chinese presidency for himself.

Señor y Señora Verea—debonair Mexicans who were celebrating their first wedding anniversary by touring the world.

Wen Shih-chen (S. T. Wen)—educator, linguist and ambassador-in-waiting, Wen was, by all accounts, the most effective Chinese negotiator.

Chapter One

THE ATTACK

In their now classic China's Response to the West, *Ssu-Yu Teng and Dr. John K. Fairbank state (page 231) that, "the decade from 1912 to 1923, since it is both recent and revolutionary, has been difficult to study. Historians have sadly neglected it."*

The British Consul at Tsinan-fu, in his intelligence report of December 1922, stated that, although there were many bandit incidents in the province, the Tientsin-Pukow Railway was trouble free and running smoothly.

2 Outrage at Lincheng

In 1924, Paul Hutchinson, a wise and articulate American missionary, reflected that "traveling in Marco Polo's day was the real thing in the way of adventure. Three and a half years from Venice to Peking! How things have changed! Fifteen days is long enough to cross the Pacific now, and it's only a couple of days from Peking to Shanghai, if the bandits don't interfere with the train schedule." [1]

May 6, 1923

Around midnight, the banjo-strumming A. L. Zimmerman concluded his impromptu concert. By 2:30 A.M., the poker game was finished, and the Chinese guards dozed where they sat. By then, even the lovers rocked in sleep through the barren, moonlit Shantung mountains. Deluxe, elegant, the Blue Express eased over a divide and crept smoothly along, until the brakes squealed and fire poured from the fields.

Yet awake, Thomas Day heard the shooting and glanced out, then woke Reginal Rowlatt. The bouncing awakened Jacobsen and Heinze. Jacobsen opened the blinds, then locked the door and grabbed some clothes. Heinze slid deep into his bunk.

No longer borne on rails, the coal-tender slid over, spilling part of its load. The baggage car fell onto its side. Several coaches sank into an awkward list, and the luxurious 'Blue' jerked to a stop, joggling passengers out of their berths. Only half awake, Lucy Aldrich peeked into the corridor, but her traveling companion, Minnie McFadden, whisked her back to safety. "They're attacking the train. . . !"²

The railway guards and some passengers fled as howling bandit hundreds converged on the crippled Express, smashing in doors with rifle butts, hacking out windows with hatchets, overrunning corridors, breaking into compartments, pushing passengers, forcing luggage, women and children screaming, rifles pistols, pandemonium.

Day and Rowlatt readied their watches, rings, and cash. Marcel Berube and J. B. Powell readied their revolvers. Lucy Aldrich slipped her family rings into her slippers.

Yellow skinned and short, tall and barefoot, some carrying candles, a bandit mob smashed their way into Major and Mrs. Pinger's compartment, beat the major, tore a ring from his finger, slapped Miriam, terrified the children, stole the luggage, and rushed on. Day and Rowlatt were roughed up and robbed, then forced off the train through a shattered window. Powell and Berube surrendered their pistols but nearly lost their fingers before they could shed their rings. Gutsy Lucy snatched Minnie McFadden's jade necklace away from one rogue, but another snatched it from her, breaking and spilling it to the floor.

Wedged in a dark corner below a lower berth, China Press reporter Lloyd Lehrbas saw many bare feet come and go as his compartment was repeatedly ransacked. Now yet another outlaw tousled the leftovers, then grappled deep beneath the bunk, then withdrew his hand and thrust in his rifle. Lloyd abandoned his Colt, crawled out, and was bullied off the train. But more bandits invaded the Pingers, again beat the major and grabbed Roland, a lad of eight. Roland Sr.

held onto his son in a wrenching tug-of-war, but wisely let go and Junior was dragged away.

Through a long, poignant interlude, Vic Haimovitch, a Shanghai broker, and hobby musician A. L. Zimmerman bided awesome time as the smashing chaos neared. When the bandits arrived, they were delighted by an awaiting king's ransom. Soon more outlaws rummaged and left. Finally one lone raider smashed in the outside window and crawled in, but the Anglos beat him senseless, climbed out the window and fled to the bush!

Ripping. Smashing. Plundering. Groups of passengers were gathered along the embankment, and some of the foreign men, forgetting their danger, chuckled at the spectacle. One Chinese passenger, an army officer, was chatting amicably with some of the marauders.

At Lincheng, but a few li—about a mile away—the emergency whistle finally shrieked. A young chieftain shouted orders, and the renegades hustled the train crew, the foreign men, women, and children, and scores of Chinese passengers into the dimly moonlit countryside. Many thieves carried luggage, clothes, rugs, mattresses, bags of food and flotsam deluxe as the soft field of sorghum graded down into a rocky ravine. Sharp stones cut the captives' bare feet, turning ankles and evaporating any remnants of humor. Now, separately hurried along the lengthening line, Major and Mrs. Pinger shouted endearments to each other until the distance between them became too great.

Terraced hills grazed by donkeys and ponies. Misses Aldrich and McFadden were offered mounts, but they refused, fearing separation. William Smith, a retired English gent, gladly climbed on, but soon tumbled off, but doggedly remounted. Shoeless, shanghaied, and shoved by impatient guards, Martha Allen painfully plodded along with Miriam and baby Edward Pinger—Robert Jr. and Major Robert Allen were . . . nowhere to be seen.

Clatter clank clunk as goodies tumbled from a bedsheet sack of booty. The bandit stooped to regather his plunder, and Lloyd Lehrbas slipped and slithered into the shadows.

Dawn. Spread out over a mile, marching three and four abreast, a strange procession perhaps a thousand strong wound its way into the countryside. Scattered here and there amidst the dull peasant garb and fraying army uniforms was a sunburst of pajamas and nightgowns, bared to the day.

A serene valley. Cultivated corn. Here they rested, and the raiders inspected their spoils. Now strapping on a wristwatch. Now trying on a hat or a dress. Now discarding some underwear or being sweet-talked out of a scarf or a pair of shoes. Some of the bandits spoke a fair English. Others knew French or pidgin. Several foreigners spoke the lingo, and some of the Chinese captives could wag several tongues. But just a respite, much too short, and soon a forced march into hill country, up a rough path with jagged flint that took its toll, even on the ponies. As Lucy plodded along, her family rings, hidden in her slippers, rubbed against her toes, each step soon bringing pain.

A deserted village. No, one solitary elder eyed this eerie exodus, and someone had set forth bean soup and kettles of tea. Not enough for all, and none for the captives. Everything was consumed without pause, and the empty vessels were carefully placed by the pathway. Onward, up, over, down, but up again. The day had grown hot when distant shots rang out. The outlaws returned the fire. Several chiefs gathered, then shouted orders. Part of the troop turned around and dashed back down the mountain to a different path around the base. A painful pace for an hour. Up they hurried, steep, rocky, up, bullets pinging wildly.

Government troops closed some ground on one of the bandit columns, but the soldiers, too, had marched all night and were less than keen. They had to slacken, had to rest. When they did, so did the bandits. Some of the captives fell asleep instantly, soon to be awakened, forced on, forced up and up until the long line began to filter through an opening into a crude fort at the crest. Here were stone walls with rifle rests. A flat acre, a vantage and control point.

Tired climbers soon filled the yard, so the headmen met and further divided their numbers, shifting most of the Chinese captives down the mountain's rear, but leaving the foreigners where they lay, nursing their bruises or fast asleep while bullets whistled high.

Gold? Pearls? One bandit clique was employing rocks to open cameras. Another man created a money or trinket-belt by hooking a brassiere around his waist. Zimmerman's banjo appeared in the booty and was randomly forced on one of the captives, who was compelled to perform a brief cacophonous symphony con bullets ricocheting!

With a revolver bobbing toward journalist Powell, one leader pressed a bilingual Chinese captive into service as a translator, then roughly dictated and dispatched via bandit messenger:

The Attack 7

General Ho
Commander Chinese Government Troops:

The chief of the "People's Self-Deliverancy Army" instructs us to write you this letter, demanding that you order your troops to cease firing at once. Otherwise the bandits will kill all foreign and Chinese captives.

J. B. Powell[3]

On a neighboring, likewise fortified hilltop, Thomas Day was also forced to write a note, then sent out with a white flag and a guard, but the firing was so intense they quickly returned. Clad in a long Roman nightshirt and proclaiming that he was the Italian vice-consul, the portly "Commodore" Guiseppe D. Musso went out to negotiate with Peking if necessary, but he, too, was forced back.

Cheers for a bandit coolie who entered the fort's rear carrying a large earthen jug of water. The brigands drank, but the captives were left parched and hungry, now separated from each other. A scorching hour, then more coolies arrived, and the foreigners were each given an egg and some water, their first nourishment since the previous evening's cuisine.

Señor y Señora Verea, debonair Mexicans on a honeymoonish world tour, had been briefly separated at the train, but had struggled and achieved reunion. Now a bandit was confronting Manuel, telling him that he, too, must play the courier. Manuel didn't at first understand, but when Jacobsen offered a translation, Señor Verea would not leave his wife. Miss Schonberg, Lucy Aldrich's French maid, was eager for the job, so she was given the note and escorted to the entrance by a Chinese who caught a bullet in the throat and collapsed dead. She made her peace and ran from the fort.

Lucy T. Aldrich opened her eyes: Chinamen all around! The man who'd awakened her produced a white collar and a pencil and, in pantomime, asked to see the Western writing-picture of "gun." Aldrich obliged, and the men hummed and marveled. One chap stepped forward with a hot water bottle. Lucy wrote the words for it. The man smiled, then pretended to drink from it. She shook her head. He started to blow it up like a balloon. Lucy mimed hot water and pain, and the new owner understood.

Slow time. Intermittent firing. Dazed silence. Muffled sobs. Once again Thomas Day was forced to pen a note. It was given to two Chinese, but they insisted that a foreigner accompany them. Tom Day Esq. was duly elected. Three hundred yards down the hill, they had to dodge for cover when several stupid bandits shot at them. Finally silence. They dashed for safety, but this time the government troops fired. Again they hugged the soil. Day jumped up and yelled, "Mei Kuo—an American coming,"[4] but the troops kept firing until the two Chinese desperately waved their coats. Then, with hands above their heads, the messengers surrendered, with luck, to freedom.

M. C. Jacobsen, of British-American Tobacco, had donated his pajama top for bandages for the women's feet. Now, barefoot and naked to the waist, bearing yet another hastily scribbled communiqué, he too ran the mountain gauntlet to the bottom where he tripped and fell, losing consciousness. Suspended reality, a fog from which he emerged to overhear two bandits discussing him. They thought him wounded, useless. In time, one crept off toward the fort. Jacobsen "played possum" until the other bandit got careless, then lunged and smashed the man and dashed for freedom. Fortunately, the government troops were not crack marksmen. Down and off came his pajama bottoms, and Jacobsen waved this flag until the guns fell silent.

Alba Coralti, Commodore Musso's editor and secretary, took hold of young Pinger's hand, but the boy's guards would not let him go. So she, two Chinese, and a Frenchman bore yet another note down into the no-man's-land, only to flee into a rice paddy when the government troops fired.

The sun flickered low in the mountains. A storm gathered and swirled in the distance, and the bandits began packing. Realizing they'd soon be marching again and that her slippers were disintegrating, Lucy Aldrich studied the landscape and secreted her heirlooms in a cleft in a rock. The path down was jagged, steep, treacherous. The bandits were jittery, hurrying, allowing no slackers. Just ahead of Lucy, an old Chinese fell. His guard cudgeled him, then shot him in the neck.

Dark, ugly copper clouds closed in as the ragamuffin army struggled down. Great explosions of thunder reverberated, then torrents of rain fell so thick that even breathing became difficult. Still they plowed on, through a watery muck near a swollen stream, passing villages without pause. Pursued again by troops, whom they occasionally heard or saw silhouetted by lightning.

The rain accumulated in the rice paddy, for it had good earthen walls and nowhere to run. Now an inch, two, three, more. Late in the night, an escaping international foursome, Alba Coralti and company, lay nearly submerged, each using the feet of another to pillow his head above water.

Stumbling, panting, drenched to the skin, Miss Lucy dragged herself along until her guard told her in English, "My wife lives in that village; you go there."[5] He pointed her to a settlement just visible in a thunderous flash.

It was a walled hamlet, and the wooden gates were chained shut. Lucy pounded on them and cried out for help, but no one heard or would answer. A straw doghouse was the only shelter. She crawled in, curled up, and later awoke soaked and shivering. Again she tried the gates, but no one would hear.

Morning. Lucy crawled from her straw cocoon and again approached the still locked entrance. Inside the compound, fifty or sixty silent, dark-complexioned men stared at her. Aldrich asked, pleaded, demanded admittance, but they were reluctant, perhaps afraid. At last the gates were opened. Lucy was searched for weapons, then an old woman led her through the courtyard to some adobe shacks and a bench where native women and children instantly swamped this "foreign-ghost," several of them touching her to see if her whiteness would rub off. The children were dirty, ragged, pitted by the pox. Some of the cow-girlie-urchins still, illegally, had bound "Lily Feet."

The women bathed Lucy's battered legs and brought noodle soup and tea. Then an old scholar in a long silken robe appeared and presented Miss Aldrich with pen and ink and a scroll onto which he'd brushed his beautiful, superannuated calligraphy. Lucy ceremoniously signed her name and address and returned the document.

The sun grew hot. With her body, a young Chinese woman gave Lucy shade. But Lucy was tired, and the friendly curious pawing was still pawing, so she persuaded a woman to take her home. She laid down in a house of adobe, but still the villagers filed in to behold her. She slept fitfully and once awoke to a room packed with silent, staring men.

They must leave—so stated a uniformed Chinese. Lucy reluctantly readied herself, gnawed by the thought that this "soldier" might be the "bandit" who had directed her to the village in the first place.

To the woman who'd fed her, to a woman who'd cradled it as a precious treasure, Lucy Aldrich had given a lace rose from her underclothes. Now a Chinese lass tied a piece of blue linen around Lucy's head, a hat against the sun. Miss Lucy mounted a mule, and she and her bandit or soldier were soon hurrying between rice paddies to . . . a bandit lair for all she knew.

Several rough miles, then another walled village. A dozen sober men stood guard on their wall, guns aimed at the strangers. Lucy's guide talked, then argued with the men, and the gates were finally opened, but the intruders were not allowed in. They were given their fill of tea, but nothing more. Later, inside another fortified hamlet, they abandoned the exhausted mule. Lucy's escort arranged for a jerry-rigged palanquin made from an old carved chair, two poles and rope. But the poles were too short, and the laborers too old, and just outside the walls they had to abandon it. Back inside they went. Lucy's kerchief wouldn't stay tied, so, in mime, she asked a woman for a safety pin. The woman had no pin, but shared precious thread and a needle.

There were no more mules. The best this guide could provide was a public taxi of sorts—a wheelbarrow. With little room to spare, Lucy sat on one side and partly behind the large wooden wheel; her companion sat similarly on the other side. An old, tired man pushed them. But he was too slow, so the guide hailed three lads from their fieldwork. With the boys in front and the old man steadying the rear, they bounced their way toward a distant smoky settlement.

Groggy from her hardships, Lucy Truman Aldrich was pleasantly stunned when her entourage entered the newly industrialized town of Tseet-sun. They halted at a tiny railway station and were instantly surrounded by joyous troops and railway men.

An employee of the Asia Development Company, an efficient though exhausted young American named Naill, took her inside.

"How much did you have to pay to get me out?" Lucy asked.

"Not one cent,"[6] said Naill, adding in a whisper that he had a fortune in his pocket just in case.

The stationmaster's wife and daughter helped clean and dress her. Then a hardy meal, a rest, and Lucy sketched a map to her hidden family rings. Later, a wicker chair was added to an old freight car, and the two Americans set out for Tsinan-fu and the Christian University Hospital. Several English-speaking Chinese army officers joined them among the bundles. The social amenities were observed, but when one officer inquired about the bandits' strength and destination, Naill touched his index finger to his lips, and Miss Lucy slipped into a dream.

"It must have been dreadful beyond words for Mrs. Allen and Mrs. Pinger to have their children torn from them in the darkness of a strange country by a wild horde of armed Chinese." [7]

Lucy Aldrich

"Odd bits of clothing were scattered all over the floor of the aisle and of the compartments. A sock here. A shoe there. Bundles of letters in another. On the floor of one coach I found a number of Mr. J. B. Powell's calling cards. Outside on the ground I later found his leather document case. Among other letters I picked up in looking for the identity of some of the passengers I did not know were two letters establishing the relationship of Miss Aldrich to Mr. John D. Rockefeller, Jr." [8]

Lloyd Lehrbas

1. Wreckage of baggage car and first class coach of the Tientsin-Pukow Blue Express, the first photo to reach America (UPI/Bettmann Newsphotos).

2. Chinese workmen clearing away wreckage after the attack (UPI/Bettmann Newsphotos).

3. Shortly after the attack (Courtesy of The Illustrated London News Picture Library).

4. On May 5, 1923, some of the gentlemen traveling First Class had enjoyed an evening of poker (Courtesy of American Car & Foundry).

5. Inside the dining car (Courtesy of American Car & Foundry).

6. Amid fine woodwork, glass and china, the passengers dined on a varied cuisine (Courtesy of American Car & Foundry).

7. Luxurious chairs and stained glass (Courtesy of American Car & Foundry).

8. Sleeping car (Courtesy of American Car & Foundry).

9. End of car (Courtesy of American Car & Foundry).

Chapter Two

HOSTAGE

The field of kaoliang was but a two-foot grass, not the ten foot stalks the hardy sorghum would be at harvest. After slithering low for forty, fifty yards, Lloyd Lehrbas rested and glanced about: dimly moonlit outlaws were hurrying toward "The Mountains Where The Bandits Live." Lloyd resumed his slow, crawling arc back toward the train and, more than once, lay inert when stragglers' voices loomed too near.

A hillock. A mound. A protecting grave where Lloyd stood and carefully surveyed the fields. No one at last, so he walked, then jogged. Later, from the rear, he cautiously approached the crippled Train de Luxe.

Short circuited lights lit the last coach. It was nearly dawn and there was no one about, but Lloyd crawled and climbed into the car's undercarriage and delicately balanced himself in the brake beams. The morning mist was soon dank. His metallic perch: awkward, cold. Perhaps he was being too careful, but then a thief hopped down and dashed to the fields, bundle in hand. Slow, chilled time, then for one harrowing moment, another bandit stooped, repacked his booty, and sauntered on.

Not long till numb. No one else appeared, so Lloyd slipped to the ground and started toward the engine. Up and into a third class coach—the windows bullet riddled and smashed. Car to car, through the demolished second class, into the mess of first where he met a badly shaken "train-boy." In frightened pidgin and sign, the man revealed his cramped, luggage rack hiding-place.

Checking several compartments, Lloyd found three more train-boys, all badly unnerved and wrapped in blankets against the cold. A rifle slung over his shoulder, a Chinese entered the car, but he wasn't a bandit, rather an official of some sort. He was followed by two, then a third, policemen with news of more foreigners several coaches back. Lloyd raced off.

Although sleepless, Carl Heinze, a German engineer from Shanghai, had weathered the ordeal in his upper berth, which he'd pulled shut. Victor Haimovitch, en route to Tientsin to ride in the horse races, and the banjoless A. L. Zimmerman had hidden in their pajamas in the fields until the debacle was complete. Now, properly attired, the gentlemen recounted their experiences and decided to poke around.

Papers and luggage littered the roadbed, and here and there they found a clue to a missing traveler's identity. Movement in the fields. White. Eerie. Someone was moving slowly toward them. The foreigners ventured forth and helped an exhausted, white-robed old Mandarin up the embankment and into a compartment where they let him rest. Then a train-boy brought pidgin bad news. Third classy. Shot. Dying or dead. A foreigner!

They followed the train-boy and found a heavy, middle-aged man with a bullet through his head. The wound was dark and ugly. The man was lifeless. Nothing could be done. Nothing. Soberly, the men resumed their investigation.

A score or more of Chinese passengers and guards who'd fled the train were returning from the fields. One passenger was wounded, as was a policeman whose rifle had exploded. Clank, chug, hiss—and an engine, tender, and boxcar backed in from Lincheng, bringing more police and railway officials. The officials only glanced about, then pulled right out again. Shots afar. But one railroad man remained and assured everyone that a relief train was on the way. More shots.

Quickening daylight. The coal tender had overturned. The third class coaches were tipped, leaning. One coach had skewed off into the fields. Nearly all the windows were smashed. Butchered luggage everywhere. But the new steel coaches had withstood the barrage hurled at them. The elegant Blue Express had inadvertently proven nearly bulletproof, and this had doubtless saved many lives.

The boxcar train once again backed in, and the four foreign men and a score of Chinese passengers pulled together whatever remnants of their belongings they could find and hoisted themselves in. Lincheng, a tidy little station, was but a few li—ten minutes away. Ten minutes, and ten, then the Peking Express chugged into Lincheng from the north. But the tracks had been severed. It could go no farther, and the remaining Blue Express passengers sought out friendship, a loan, a meal, some clothes, sleep.

At noon, there were cheers and celebration when Martha Allen and Miriam and baby Edward Pinger waddled into Lincheng in an ox-cart under police escort. Two ladies from the Peking Express took charge, brought the exhausted women to their compartment, found clothes, and ordered food. Dr. Friedlander (also identified as Dr. Fernbach), a physician en route to Shanghai, tended to their bruises, and Lloyd Lehrbas listened in as the women wept over their missing loved ones and the agonizing march. But the women needed rest, so Lloyd strolled about the train and station, and met an aging priest who was doctoring some of the injured Chinese.

"The railroad should arrange to get their trains through here during daylight," said Father William Lenfers, a German missionary who'd lived in the province many years. "The entire district is infested with bandits, and it is not safe."[1]

In no hurry, a second train eased into Lincheng, and the Blue Express passengers were told they'd soon be able to complete their journey north. Lloyd Lehrbas, however, decided instead to return to Shanghai, home base of the China Press, and file his firsthand report of the attack. He rode the Peking Express as far as the wreck, where all southbound passengers had to detrain, walk around the ravaged liner, then board another train that had come from the south.

Meanwhile, Paul P. Whitham of Asia Development had gone to meet the Blue Express at the Tsinan railway station, the original destination for J. B. Powell, Lloyd Lehrbas, and Kang Tung-yi, Sunday editor of the newspaper Shun Pao. These noted journalists were to join Dr. Jacob Gould Schurman, the American Minister, and various dignitaries on an inspection tour of some repair work on the Yellow River dike. But the train was delayed, and there was talk of a holdup. Whitham went to the American consulate and asked for any news. Vice-consul Milbourne hadn't heard anything but phoned the civil and military governors' offices, but they could shed no light on the matter. Whitham then returned to the depot and learned that a repair train was being assembled. He called in two of his agents, Naill and Weisenberg, and told them to ride down and "telegraph back their findings."[2]

While the Chinese authorities surveyed the damage and began their cleanup, Naill and Weisenberg likewise viewed the wreck. In the dead man's compartment they found the briefcase and papers of one Joseph Rothman. The compartment also yielded two pistols and enough ammunition for a small war. They telegraphed in their findings:

> Twenty-six foreigners held by bandits. Powell in hands of bandits. Larry Lehrbas, China Press, arrive Tsinan tonight. Rothman, Britisher, killed. Information meager. Will stay here till tomorrow.[3]

Dr. Schurman notified the Shanghai consulate and the Peking Legation and informed Washington. Meanwhile, the consul staff met the first victims to reach Tientsin. Martha Allen and the Pingers were taken to the American Forces

Hospital, and the other passengers gave sworn statements on what they knew about their missing fellow travelers.

Before long, a second mercy train reached Tientsin. Day and Jacobsen, who weren't seriously hurt, continued their journey north, but Misses Schonberg and McFadden were driven to the Shantung Christian University Hospital, where the ambassador would later visit them. Dr. Schurman also telegraphed strongman Tsao Kun and demanded immediate action. Meanwhile, more telegrams poured in from Naill and Weisenberg:

> Leaving for bandit outpost with French and Italian Consuls General. Wu Chang-chi putting every possible obstacle in our path. Can secure immediate release of foreigners if we secure proper cooperation from military. Military does not want to negotiate with bandits.[4]

> Soldiers pursuing bandits over hills. All foreigners almost dead due to long marches and no food. Within three days all foreigners will die unless negotiation is effected. For God's sake do something.[5]

Chapter Three

FOREIGN MEDDLING

"One need not be obsessed with the merits of the Chinese to recognize that the organization of their empire is in truth the best that the world has ever seen."[1]

Voltaire, 1764

"What China needs is righteousness, and in order to attain it, it is absolutely necessary that she have a knowledge of God and a new conception of man, as well as of the relation of man to God. She needs a new life in every individual soul, in the family, and in society. The manifold needs

of China we find, then, to be a single imperative need. It will be met permanently, completely, only by Christian civilization."[2]

Arthur H. Smith, 1894

Tibetans, Arabs, Romans, Japanese, Indians, northern barbarians and multifarious foreigners have, since chronicles were kept, always sought trade, succor, adventure in the "Flowery Kingdom" of China. In the seventh Christian century, the heretical Nestorians found tolerance, built shrines, "laughed their cryings and did their dance,"[3] then utterly vanished, leaving but one stone tablet to be unearthed nearly a millennium later.

In 1275, Marco Polo found Cathay, served the emperor, and later spent enough time in Italian debtors' prison to record his untenable tale. In the early 1500s, the swashbuckling Portuguese arrived, but they were soon quarantined at Macao. Jesuit missionaries followed, bringing European math and science, dedication and persistence, and an ecclesiastical soporific custom tailored for an educated Chinese elite.

During the last decadent years of the Ming, these suave Jesuits were invited to Peking where they engaged in sophisticated debate, made high-ranking converts, revised the Imperial Calendar, and wrote some 380 works in Chinese. Father Verbiest demonstrated his command of Christian canons by mustering the names of three hundred saints, one per cannon he cast. When the barbarous Manchus captured the northern capital in 1644, they saw no need to oust these educated courtiers, so the Jesuits stayed on as "astronomers, interpreters, cartographers, painters, engravers, architects . . . engineers."[4]

For nearly a century, the Society of Jesus enjoyed an exclusive Christian voice in China and a monopoly over the interpretation of the Orient to a small, literate European community. Then came dissension. Portugal was reluctant to surrender her monopoly on Chinese evangelism, but France and Rome wanted to expand their influence. Dominican, Franciscan, and Augustinian monks appeared and started preaching in the streets in direct contravention of Chinese propriety and law. With equal zeal, these new monks attacked the Jesuits for indulging in "theological compromises."

While the Society of Jesus had chosen to overlook Chinese "ancestor worship," to these new priests, bowing before the family alter was an intolerable act of pagan worship. There was also a tremendous furor over what name "the All-Just, the All-Righteous, the All-Good . . . Merciful . . . Forgiving . . . Truthful . . . Loving"[5] Christian God Almighty should be called in Chinese.

To the Jesuits, the names T'ien or Shang-ti were perfectly acceptable. To the Dominicans, it seemed important that God's name not be T'ien but T'ien-chu. To the Chinese, it all probably seemed like so much nettlesome nitpicking. The emperor, who valued his Jesuits, sent a collection of documents to Rome in their support, but the Pope replied with an unfavorable bull. Papal delegates crisscrossed the globe. Bull followed bull. The Jesuits were denounced, and the K'ang-hsi emperor was offended. Although individual priests would maintain the Imperial Calendar and serve other technical functions at Court, the missionaries' role would be one of progressively diminishing importance.

At Canton, there was erratic trade with the British, Dutch, Portuguese, and others. This commerce was finally dominated by the British East India Company, which first sought a wide range of Chinese miscellanea, then specialized in silks and teas. But the Chinese spun the web. Western trade was relegated to one port only, the one "farthest from Peking,"[6] and even there the foreigners were segregated and kept outside the city walls, in the "thirteen factories."

Since tropical Canton had little use for England's warm woolens, the British company had chronic difficulty "balancing" this trade. The solution was to import raw cotton, silver, and the muddy brown sap of the Bengal poppy from India "to make one part of Britain's Asia trade pay for the other."[7]

This "Canton System" produced a century of relatively peaceful and profitable trade totally devoid of "relations between the English and Chinese governments,"[8] and equally lacking in cultural or intellectual intercourse. But the English were nearly addicted to tea, and the British Empire was prospering and seeking additional outlets for its products. Thus, in 1793, King George III (of Boston Tea Party fame) dispatched the Earl of Macartney and a massive entourage to the Chinese capital in a quest for diplomatic equality, additional ports-of-entry, and a regular printed tariff to replace the informal "squeeze" being exacted by the local mandarins. This huge delegation "brought magnificent presents in 600 packages which were finally carried into Peking by 90 wagons, 40 barrows, 200 horses and 3000 coolies."[9]

Duly labeled as "tribute" by the blasé Chinese bureaucrats, these offerings were shuffled along to the palaces' storerooms, and although the Chinese emperor did complement King George for his "respectful spirit of submission," no boons were granted.[10]

But even without official sanction, the volume and nature of this commerce was changing. In London, there was an organized howl against the East India monopoly. In Canton, interlopers, independent agents, and sundry rogues made quick fortunes by selling "foreign mud." They imported a thousand chests per year by the late 1700s. By 1838, forty thousand chests of 133 pounds each were entering the country. Some 160 million opium grams so that two to ten million Chinese heads and countless silver taels could float away in smoke.

Opium's huge profits tempted the squeezed and squeezing Mandarins, so the trade flourished and moved inland and up the coast. The Forbidden City finally took notice; a scholarly debate ensued, and the emperor decreed that this fetid trade must cease.

It took two months by canal boat and palanquin for Commissioner Lin to reach Canton from Peking. Accelerating a recent crackdown, he quickly destroyed the Chinese dens, dealers, and distributors, then turned his statecraft on the foreigners. He delicately deprived them of their servants, blockaded them into their "factories," demanded their "mud," and penned his righteous indignation to Victoria Ying-kuo Wang, "the ruler of England."[11]

The British Superintendent of Trade, Captain Charles Elliot, collected 20,183 chests of opium from the gathered multinational merchants and, on behalf of his government, surrendered it to the Chinese authorities. This massive muck was "publicly and spectacularly destroyed,"[12] and the cogs of the British Empire's war machine clanged into high gear.

Arguing against a swelling tide, William Gladstone addressed his fellow parliamentarians thus:

> You will be called upon, even if you escape from condemnation on this motion, to show cause for your present intention of making war upon the Chinese. They gave us notice to abandon the contraband trade. When they found that we would not, they had the right to drive us from their shores on account of our obstinacy in persisting in this infamous and atrocious traffic. I am not competent to judge how long this war may last, but this I can say, that a war more unjust in its origin, a war more calculated in its progress to cover this country with permanent disgrace, I do not know of. . . .[13]

But the armada sailed, and, after three years of intermittent coastal warfare, the Manchus, with their antiquated weaponry, were beaten. China surrendered Hong Kong, agreed to "open" four more ports and to publish a tariff, and was saddled with a huge indemnity to cover the costs of the war, and, said the treaty, "the value of the opium which was delivered up in Canton in the Month of March 1839. . . ."[14]

Riding these British coattails, the French secured trading rights and, by stealth, got Christianity removed from a Chinese list of subversive organizations; the Americans got "without a struggle all the privileges that Britain had fought for."[15]

26 *Outrage at Lincheng*

The profits of the "China Trade," increasingly the opium trade, were so vast that virtually every foreign merchant in Canton wallowed in it. Some enterprising Yankee traders so monopolized the importation of Turkish "mud" "that many Chinese concluded that Turkey must be a part of the United States."[16]

In 1856, with minuscule provocation, the French and British struck again in hostilities now called the Arrow War. When Peking again capitulated, opium was legalized, more indemnities were heaped on, and the whole of China was effectively "opened" to foreign penetration.

The Russians, who'd occasionally been active in Mongolia and Siberia, took a nice, ice-free hunk of treaty-pie. The United States, Prussia, Denmark, the Netherlands, Spain, Belgium, Italy, Austria-Hungary, and others all forged treaties with the Chinese during the 1860s.[17]

To frustrate the Chinese "squeeze," to enforce "free trade," and to facilitate extracting the enormous cash indemnities out of the vanquished kingdom, the British extended their recently formed Maritime Customs Service to another nine, newly opened ports. As more murky fortunes were made, the Western nations magnanimously turned "from coercion to cooperation with the Dynasty."[18]

The easing of restrictions against Christianity brought an increase in missionary activity. Long established in the interior, Catholic priests revived sleeping churches, erected schools, and made innumerable converts, now from the lower echelons of society.

Along the coast, Protestant proselytizers founded schools and clinics and did pioneer work in translation, but made exasperatingly few converts. After traveling halfway around the globe, these often mini-minded men plied China's waterways on armed opium transports, bringing the "heathen Chinee" a sadly ruthless diatribe against his entire ancient civilization. When a French consul, ten nuns, and another ten foreigners were massacred at Tientsin in 1870, the thin veneer of international cooperation crumbled.

Throughout the 1870s, the Western nations tracked their "mud" into and consolidated their control over China's vassal kingdoms. Japan, newly "opened" or reopened only a generation earlier, was quick to modernize and joined in the melee. When French, then American gunboats failed to "open" Korea, Japanese warships finally forced this "Hermit Kingdom" to relegate two coastal cities to trade.

In 1876, the Jardine-Matheson Company, without the approval of any Chinese officials whatsoever, built the Shanghai-Wusung Railroad, China's first. In the northwest, the Russians were nipping at Chinese Turkestan. In the south, the British were absorbing Burma.

France, in 1874, forced a treaty on the Vietnamese and claimed sovereignty over that nation. But the Vietnamese nation of Annam had been a Chinese province for a thousand years before gaining independence, and the two countries had remained intimately interwoven. When the French became too obstreperous, the Vietnamese invited the Chinese in to drive them out. Between 1883 and 1885, a Sino-French war raged, and China lost another jewel from her mud-stained cape.

Throughout the 1880s, Korea was also embroiled in intrigue as various Western nations snatched treaty rights or vied for political control. In 1882, Chinese and Japanese troops clashed, but Japan backed away from war. Along with Russia, Britain, and the United States, Japan continued to force intercourse on this reluctant "Hermit Kingdom." When a rebellion erupted in 1892, Japan again sent in troops, and the Flowery Kingdom and the Land of the Rising Sun plunged into war. Within a few months, the Japanese had demolished China's virgin fleet and whipped the Celestial Empire.

For all her vastness and her population of millions, colossal China was revealed as a weak and tired paper-tiger, and the Western powers now leapt in for a glorious colonial grab. The French pushed into southwest China from Vietnam. Germany grabbed Kaichow and spread into Shantung. Russia took Port Arthur and part of Manchuria. Britain extended Hong Kong, secured a northern naval base, and consolidated her control over the Yangtze Valley. Even Italy launched a fleet.

Obstinately and successfully for more than thirty years, the Chinese scholar-officials had obstructed all plans of foreign powers to drive into China through the railways. In 1896, there were a mere 240 miles of track in the entire land. After the great "scramble of '98," the foreigners sketched another five thousand miles worth of track across the turbulent, crumbling kingdom.

Rabidly anti-foreign, the "Righteous and Harmonious Fists" was not a clandestine gymnastic organization. Nor was the "Boxer Rebellion" essentially a rebellion. However, in Chihli and Shantung provinces in 1899 and 1900, there was a massive, gory uprising. Starving peasants and embittered boatmen whose livelihoods had been smashed by Western steamships found a scapegoat in all-things-foreign, but especially in Christianity, whose proponents had often demonstrated a pomposity directly proportional to the steadily increasing presence of foreign gunboats. Decades of suppressed rage exploded, and half-crazed Boxer bands butchered Chinese Christians en masse and slaughtered the imported variety by the score.

The Manchu court vacillated between mild suppression and covert encouragement before siding with the Boxers and ordering the government troops to drive the foreign devils into the sea. The legations at Peking and Tientsin were surrounded, communications were cut, and the Manchus declared war on perhaps half the "civilized world."

British, American, French, German, Belgium, Italian, Russian, and Japanese troops battled their way inland from the coast, relieved Tientsin, broke the siege at Peking, ravaged the city, mopped up any pockets of resistance, and then turned a savage eye toward peace. The "Boxer Protocol" of 1901, a supermarket list of condemnations combined with a colossal cash indemnity, would yoke the Chinese for the next forty years. With these treaties, concessions, leases, loans, banks, maritime customs, gunboats and troops firmly in place, the Western powers combined in various consortia to lay track, carve tunnels, build bridges, and ramrod a belated Railroad Age into China's fecund innards.

Germany and Britain, in 1898, jointly secured a concession to build Shantung's Tientsin-Pukow Railway, but further negotiations were broken off because of the Boxer troubles. Only in 1908 was the final agreement concluded, and construction was begun the following year. The Germans in the north. The British in the south. But these two empires were already clashing, and this rivalry insured that the Chinese got generous terms, but also that Americans got contracts. The German section opened in February 1912, and the British slice was finished in June. Soon thereafter, a fanatical Serbian shot the Archduke Ferdinand and the Europeans suddenly turned inward for a gay little august war that surely would be over before Christmas!

China quickly declared her neutrality, possibly hoping to be ignored, but such was not to be. Japan declared war on Germany, invaded Shantung province, grabbed up the Kaiser's holdings, and handed the Chinese twenty-one "secret" demands that would have made China a mere Japanese puppet-state. But China leaked this blackmail to the outside world, and international pressure convinced Japan to content herself with Shantung, plus parts of Manchuria and Siberia.

Woodrow Wilson might have once envisioned an amicable settlement to this hideous Great War, but his European Allies, having borne the brunt of the horrific carnage, were much more inclined to pulverize Germany and see that she would never rise from the ashes. Thus gaping wounds, conflicting visions, secret deals, and plain old greed turned the Treaty of Versailles into a mass of compromise. It was neither devastating nor serene. The farsighted Marshal Foch called this "peace treaty" a twenty year armistice. It held out no hope for Ho Chi Minh, and the honorable Chinese delegation could not, from pride and fear for their lives, even affix their names thereto. The "Ally" China had once again been slashed: her sacred Shantung province had been left in Japanese hands. A "May 4th" patriotic rage swept the uncentered, Middle Kingdom.

The First World War had changed everything, or nothing, or had "significantly altered the balance of power in the Far East, a situation which was largely ignored by the Versailles Peace settlements."[19] Britain was exhausted and soon wracked with unemployment, and had lost relative stature in Asia, if only because Japan and the United States had emerged stronger there. A temporarily harsh peace settled over Europe, but, in Siberia and the Far East, swashbucklers were still slashing. Consequently, another major international peace conference was convened in Washington in the autumn of 1921.

Jacob Gould Schurman had first touched Chinese soil in 1899 as chief of a commission studying the Philippine Islands in the wake of the Spanish-American War. Following a distinguished tenure as president of Cornell University, Dr. Schurman joined his friend Charles Evans Hughes in campaigning for the election of Warren G. Harding to the American presidency. After Harding's victory, Hughes was appointed Secretary of State, and the eminently qualified Schurman was confirmed as Minister to China. On August 24, 1921, Dr. Schurman arrived in Shanghai and was soon "busy compiling a detailed report of his observations in China which he apparently believed would enlighten and shape the work of the conference."[20]

The gargantuan Washington Conference was convened to tactfully terminate a British-Japanese military alliance, to limit an exhaustive naval arms race, and to better define certain "spheres of influence." Dr. Schurman's long cables and China's aspirations were accorded perhaps a yawn.

However, China and Japan were strongly encouraged to settle the mode and amount of payment Japan would receive for the improvements she'd made to Shantung's railroads. When a stiff bargain was sealed, Japan agreed to vacate the province into which Confucius had been born.

Although the Chinese delegation achieved a limited success in Washington, conditions at home continued to deteriorate. In mid December, Chang Tso-lin—the warlord of Manchuria—marched his army into Peking and dictated a cabinet to his own liking. By April, the opposing Chihli forces had regrouped, and civil war was nipping at the capital. Conditions in Hunan province grew so bad that there was a general exodus of foreigners. Then, in December 1922, an incident occured that seriously jeopardized Sino-American relations.

Heavily laden with silver, Charles Coltman, in a four-car caravan including the American consul, was stopped at a military checkpoint at Kalgan. A Chinese officer informed the party of a sparkling new order from the military governor forbidding the removal of all but small amounts of hard currency, and he denied them passage. Consul Sokobin objected, but the officer "restated his orders" and "instructed the members of the guard to load their rifles."[21] Sokobin demanded to see a commanding officer, but the local commissioner only reaffirmed the embargo. The consul returned to the caravan and, after discussion, the party apparently decided to . . . bluff the blockade? But the soldiers fired, Coltman was hit, dying three days later, and "the western press in China called for foreign intervention to punish China."[22]

On January 3, 1923, Schurman presented Minister Wang with six demands:

> 1. an apology from the Chinese Government to the American Government; 2. an apology from the Military Governor at Kalgan to the American Consul who was to approve in advance the form and terms of the apology; 3. the summary dismissal of the Chief of Staff of the Military Governor, the chief adjutant and the third officer present at the guard station, and the punishment of these officers according to the maximum penalties prescribed by law; 4. an indemnity for the family of Coltman as determined by the American Government; 5. an end to the ban on transportation of currency by Americans as authorized by treaty rights; 6. the right of American merchants to present claims for damages resulting from interruption of their commercial business. The Chinese Government gave no immediate response.[23]

As the days, weeks, and months passed, Dr. Schurman met with the new acting foreign minister, twice with the premier, once with "Christian General" Feng, then once again with the foreign minister. Somehow the demands became obscured. The Chinese preferred to pay a "compassionate allowance as evidence of sympathy"[24] rather than an "indemnity," and there was little hope of getting the military governor, General Chang Hsi-yuan, to apologize to "an officer of lower rank."[25]

In mid-April, the American minister met with Wellington Koo, the foreign minister designate. The Coltman caper was brought to the attention of President Li Yuan-hung and Tsao Kun, the power behind the throne.

On April 30, Schurman went to Pao-ting and had a five hour conversation with General Tsao Kun. The two men agreed to have General Chang Hsi-yuan apologize to the Minister at the legation within a week. Tsao gave his assurance, stating that Chang was one of his subordinates. On May 5, 1923, General Chang Hsi-yuan presented himself to the American Legation and apologized to Schurman as the official responsible for the men of his command who shot and killed Charles Coltman. . . .

Schurman successfully resolved a difficult incident that seriously jeopardized American-Chinese relations. The settlement of the Charles Coltman incident, however, did not give Schurman a respite from such strained diplomacy, for on the night of May 5-6, the day that General Chang Hsi-yuan apologized, bandits wrecked a train and kidnapped American hostages.[26]

Chapter Four

"IT'S MUSSO AND I THINK HE'S DEAD!"

"The march from the train would have been worth a million to an American movie director. Most of the male passengers took the thing humorously, expecting to be taken but a short distance away while the work of rifling the train was completed. As we now know, this expectation was not realized." [1]

J. B. Powell

36   *Outrage at Lincheng*

"I now bent every effort to overtake Junior. As light dawned, bullets began to fly and the bandits separated into at least two columns, each taking part of the prisoners. The mental agony and physical pain which I had already suffered was augmented by the fear that I might not overtake the boy. After about five hours, however, luck was with me, and almost exhausted, I joined him.

All that day we were under fire, which coming from both the east and south, made it difficult to secure dependable cover. Our only food for over thirty five hours was one hardboiled egg, some bread resembling wrapping paper and a little lukewarm or hot water already contaminated by dozens of bandit lips.

With nightfall came a severe hail and rain storm. Under its cover, we plunged down the mountain and with but a short stop at a small village, made a forced march which at daylight found me utterly exhausted."[2]

R. W. Pinger

Led atop a donkey in torrential rain, Minnie McFadden was culled from the main group, taken into a soggy field, and soon lost in mist. Half a night's trudging brought the ragamuffin army to an abandoned village, where the foreigners were held in a pig pen. After only a brief rest, the hostages were shaken from their slumber, herded together, forced on, over narrow footpaths, nearly till dawn, to a corral in a village near a mountain.

The frightening, occasional gunshots were cleaning mishaps, not aimed at troops, hostages, or brother brigands who tinkered with their loot, picked lice, drank wine, chatted, or slept with stoic bellies empty. Bobby Allen, king of his dozen years, was famished, so Major Allen and J. B. Powell cajoled one raider into finding some tea and sardines for the lad. But what one bandit can give, two others can covet and take half away.

Mustered around the corral, readying themselves for yet another awesome promenade, the dazed and sleepy Anglos demanded to know where the women were.

"No have got,"[3] replied one of the outlaws.

Sharply tailored in a man's suit, Señora Verea announced that the bandits had taken the women away in the night. They'd tried to make her go, but she wouldn't leave her husband, her Manuel!

They soon scrambled up another mountain, then down. Then up, and from the crest: a glimpse of distant trailing troops. Up and down on empty stomachs, dangerous walkways, injured feet. Commodore Musso was limping badly.

Dark exhaustion in a long dark hut. A score of foreign and several bilingual Chinese captives lay there, nursing their bruises, dozing, chatting. Voices approached, stopped at the door, then departed. Big Leon Friedman, an auto dealer from Shanghai, investigated. A body lay on an improvised litter. "It's Musso and I think he's dead!"[4] Friedman found a pulse, and they carted him in. While stumbling along without his glasses, the Commodore had fallen and injured his spine.

Too soon dawn. Musso was loaded onto a stretcher of poles and straw, and off they marched, eating little or nothing rather than Shantung dog, or tortillas filled with scorpions, their stingers removed. Morning, noon, and night, they zigzagged into the rugged highlands. William Smith, a sprightly old tourist dressed in blue pajamas, tackled his companions' grumblings with a vintage British stiff upper lip.

Here and there were villages, some friendly, others hungry and disinterested. A few were deserted, spoiled by the wars, looted of cups and a teapot not by Orientals. Outside one guarded hamlet, the bandits traded money and jewels for opium's haze.

Down, deep down into a long valley three-to-ten miles wide. Friendly turf, so the outlaws established lookouts and dispersed. Major Robert Allen of the U.S. Army in Manila, the Frenchman Emile Gensburger, his cousins Fred and Eddie Elias, their friend Theo Saphiere, and Dr. Siji C. Hung were bivouacked near the bandits' headquarters. A few li away, Lee Solomon, Reginal Rowlatt, the elderly Smith, Marcel Berube of the salt monopoly, and Major Roland Pinger were forced into a vermin-infested barn. Señor and Señora Verea were held in a third camp, and the remaining cream of the hostages—Musso, Friedman, Henley, Powell, K. P. Koo, and Cheng Chi—received the best accommodations as "guests" of the crumbling "Dragon Door Temple." There, a handful of ragged devotees smiled upon the freebooters who had, the previous year, donated generously toward repairs.

Under the lax gaze of several guards and the wide-eyed stares of a few farmers, the hostages were soon reveling in a bath and washing their clothes in a sparkling stream alongside this mountain shrine. Word of the "foreign devils" spread quickly, and scores of natives flocked to view these fabled alien beings as they frolicked in a stream from which

Kung Ch'iu, known as Master Kung, Kung the Philosopher or Confucius, was said to have sipped.

A dozen alert and cautious bandits entered the agreed upon village and ordered the old priest to follow them. They climbed over the mountain, then clambered down into a renegade settlement where sundry farmers knew this kindly missionary. Some hid in shame.

A room had been cleaned and prepared. Etiquette and propriety were strictly observed. Father Lenfers was given an honorable seat. A handful of headmen took their places, showing great deference to their commander-in-chief, a well dressed young man who, on this day, called himself Wang. Wang said his men were not bandits but soldiers who'd been discharged without receiving their pay. He then outlined his demands: the surrounding troops must be withdrawn; his men must be reinstated in the army; there must be no reprisals . . . .

Father Lenfers could not promise these things, but only try to soothe and soften. But the headmen were uncompromising, so the priest asked to see the captives. Leon Friedman and Eddie Elias were escorted in. Both men were sunburned but otherwise well, gratified by the priest's efforts and for the several letters he'd carried in. Major Allen entered and was greatly cheered by the news that his wife was safe. Fred Elias joined the crew—carried in on a stretcher, his right leg infected and swollen, but in good spirits. Lenfers told the men of the growing rescue operation and offered what solace he could. While the captives read their mail or dashed off hasty letters, the aging missionary and the headmen again sat and haggled in the native tongue.

Wang was "quiet toned, cordial, friendly, grim," saying that if his demands weren't met in two, maybe three days, he would kill all the hostages. "Do not deceive yourself or think me soft," he warned. "What I threaten I will carry out exactly as I promise."[5] Wang gave the priest a communiqué and suggested that he best be on his way.

Father Lenfers asked to see Commodore Musso, but Musso was sick and miles away. Lenfers then pleaded to be allowed to bring out Major Allen. Part of the prearranged deal was that Father Lenfers would be allowed to bring out six prisoners. But a bandit runner had arrived with news of another troop train, so the outlaws would free no one. The priest was given a guide and sent away. Back over the narrow footpaths, soon alone, abandoned, hour after hour, seemingly endless li, he pushed his old body until he hobbled into Lincheng where he delivered his letters.

> To the various foreign consuls:
>
> In the ninth year of the republic, 1920, we were defeated in Hunan and lost our position. We then returned to our respective native places and resumed our not forgotten occupation as agriculturists.
> Now the fifth and sixth brigades are daily pursuing us, claiming that we are bandit. We are therefore compelled to gather our men in the mountains in order to wait for peace.
> During the past few years, the people in the adjacent villages have been greatly oppressed by both sides, that is, bandit and troops, [while] ostensibly the troops were sent to suppress the bandit, they have robbed the people of their money and have carried away specially cattle and horses.

The people, on account of their inability to live in peace, have joined us in large numbers.

The foreign captives are still here. It is desired at present that all troops which surround us be immediately withdrawn to the provincial capital. We will then discuss our other demands. If the troops are not withdrawn within two days, all foreigners will be shot and no one will be spared. The military officers should take action.

Self Governed Army for the Establishment
of the Country.

Sun, Commander in Chief[6]

Several soldiers of this "Self Governed Army" brought their temple captives a large cut of pork. The foreigners happily scrounged up a pan, built a fire, found some wild garlic, and brewed up an excellent broth. The meat, however, was rather tough, so they let it simmer while they tended to their feet, chatted, or napped. When they returned for their feast, it was gone, stolen. An irate delegation was sent to discuss the matter with "Commander Sun," a leader among the chiefs.

Young, intelligent, and able in English, Sun Mei-yao was not unkind. He patiently heard the captives' lament, then explained that his brothers had been hungry a long time. If the government troops didn't stop chasing them, a time might come when they would no longer be able to feed their hostages. They might instead have to eat them.[7]

But with the opening of talks, it was not necessary for the bandits to gobble their catch, and the captives' lot quickly improved. The Reverend Carroll Yerkes, of the American

Presbyterian Mission, shipped in several well-cured hams and soon thereafter a Good Book for each and every captive.

Quipped Leon Friedman, contemplating these developments: "First we starve and the missionary sends us ham. Then when we want something to read, he sends us the New Testament. What's a Jew supposed to do . . . ?"[8]

A bizarre postal service—"The Bandit Express"—sprang into being as local coolies plied the rugged paths between the bandit camps and the fortified coal mines at Tsaochuang. The Red Cross, the Shanghai Chamber of Commerce, the Tientsin-Pukow Railway, the Chinese and American military all rushed in foodstuffs and supplies. Carl Crow, businessman and author, arrived with suitcases stuffed with food, letters, and packages from family members. Bypassing "channels," Crow hired some native bearers and began shipping goodies into the wilderness. Thus, heavily laden coolies began intermittently to penetrate the bandit lair, bringing, as agreed, rice for the outlaws, but bread, crackers, canned milk, sardines, bully beef, bottled water, raisins, fruit, vegetables, and tobacco for the foreigners. The outlaws glanced for hidden extras, but surrendered most of this cache to their now "honored guests."

On May 9, Yang Ssu-hsiang, a Blue Express passenger who'd been freed because he'd served in the army with some of the outlaws, met with his former associates and convinced them that, if they wanted to keep their heads, they had best free the American kids. Yang escorted the lads to the mines and passed them on to General Ho.

China-born businessman, linguist, and paladin, Roy Anderson arrived on May 10 to collect the boys, but Ho Feng-yu would not surrender custody without a proper receipt. The unflappable Anderson duly acknowledged receiving from "the gentleman on the hill who was in command of an apparently independent organization which included some men who were wearing Chinese uniform, two American boys in behalf of their parents with thanks."[9] Major Horsfall took the lads north on the first train.

Carrying letters and another bandit communiqué, Jerome Henley and an interpreter emerged from the hills on May 11, on a twenty-four hour "parole." He got a festive welcome from diplomats, military authorities, friends, family, and reporters who had converged on the fortified compound. Henley was treated to an indulgent bath, an elaborate meal, and a multitude of questions. At dawn, he went back into the bush with several special companions.

Roy Anderson was quite at home in the Flowery Kingdom in his khaki, his pith helmet and riding boots. His associate was a polished, mysterious Chinese gentleman. With proper pomp, savoir-faire, and "face," this party entered the bandit domain, appropriately chaired by native bearers.

Lookouts had long followed their approach, and the outlaws had prepared a sumptuous table. Only after dining would the bandits speak to the business at hand. The surrounding troops must be withdrawn; their men must be reinstated in the army; and the foreign powers must guarantee any agreement.

After two days of hard bargaining, a delicate arrangement was agreed to whereby when .. but .. as .. who? Dark. An hour before dawn, the foreigners were awakened and told to get ready. Musso was lifted into a sedan chair, and the outlaw army was again on the move, seven miles through the valley, up in tattered footwear and bare feet, over a divide, down into a peaceful glen, poppies in rows along the pathway. Finally a derelict village where they laid over for the night.

In the morning, the captives were twice told to get ready, only to have the order canceled. In the afternoon they decamped, and in the confusion, K. P. Koo from Nanking's Teacher's College and a train guard named Da Hu escaped. They weren't missed. If anything, the outlaws were increasing in number, gaining recruits who'd heard of the great coup!

Several level miles, then up a narrow pathway. Up and up more. To the crest where the bandits sang, "Pao Tzu Ku! Pao Tzu Ku!" Conical, volcanic, the highest mountain yet, and its nearing sight brought song.

They labored down into a wide, nearly barren, gradually narrowing valley. Here and there were joyous lookouts, and sundry bandits broke ranks, taking groups of Chinese prisoners with them. But the main body kept moving, again uphill. The valley narrowed until it was no more than a ravine between two ridges. Up they clambered into a tattered hamlet and a hero's welcome, and more of the outlaws scattered. The main group, though, kept moving, through the village, into an arbor, through the woods to steps chiseled in stone, and up they climbed. At last, they passed through a pailow—an arch of honor—and entered a cloistered plateau.

Five sturdy stone buildings on a flat acre, encircled by impossible cliffs. All empty, save several smiling Buddhas. Guarded by many, sixteen foreigners and eight bilingual

"It's Musso and I think he's dead!"

Chinese captives finally rested. There were yet some canned goods. Soon dusk. The hostages were ordered into the main temple, forced to bow to the idol, and then left to bed-down on the cold ground amid bandit coolies, cooties, centipedes, fleas, lizards, scorpions, and trepidations.

Chapter Five

"THE BANDITS LOOKED AND BEHAVED LIKE SOLDIERS."

"The bandits looked and behaved like soldiers. Well disciplined. Commands passed along lines in a military way. They had parts of uniforms. . . . Others were just ordinary farmers."[1]

M. C. Jacobsen

The first group, the professional bandits, although they are undoubtedly in the minority, have existed in China and particularly in this part of China for centuries. They are inferior to the second group not only in numbers but also in intelligence, and are hardly capable of conceiving and executing such an affair as the Lincheng outrage. A fairly efficient Chinese police force would have no difficulty in keeping this group within bounds if it were deprived of the support of the second group.

As to the second, in the course of negotiation here it has been learned that among this group are the following: [1] Discharged soldiers of Chang Chin-yao, Chang Hsun and other former military commanders, [2] soldiers who fled from Chang Tso-lin's forces upon their defeat by Wu Pei-fu in 1922, [3] At least one former soldier of the Bolshevik army in Siberia, [4] coolies who were in France or in the French or British coolie corps, [5] at least one criminal refugee, [6] members of the Kuomintang, [7] several men whose near relatives had been killed by the provincial officials, [8] At least one, whose wife had been captured by bandits and joined their ranks in order to remain near her, [9] many whose lot had become so miserable at home because of poor wages and the generally unsatisfactory conditions under the present government of China that they had taken affairs into their own hands by joining the bandits, [10] Many military deserters, long without pay, who, having outgrown their days of usefulness as laborers, have fallen into this semi-military occupation of banditry to gain an easy living.

Other classes would undoubtedly be found if a census of the entire group could be taken, but I believe that the great majority come under the above or similar heads.[2]

Wallace Philoon
U.S. Assistant Military Attaché

One fellow, whom we called "Monkey Face," had been a bandit for five years. According to his story, the bandits had raided his father's home near the railway about fifty miles distant and had carried him and his brothers and sisters into captivity. His sisters were sold into slavery, and he and his brothers, in order to save their own lives, had joined the bandit gang. "Monkey Face's" ambition in life was to become a soldier and so fare less hard. . . .

Then there was a very interesting chap whom we called "Rusky." He had become the personal servant of a Russian officer stationed in China away back before the war . . . and accompanied his master in campaigns on the German front. After the Russian blowup, he joined the Bolshevist army and served in Siberia. He claimed to have participated in several Bolshevist raids along the Chinese Eastern Railway and into Mongolia. After the Japanese troops had evacuated Vladivostok and things had settled down in Siberia, he deserted and came back to his old home in Shantung Province . . . . He was always very kind and helpful to members of our party . . . .

One old fellow who earned our profoundest respect, or rather whom all of us most feared, was named "Po-po Liu." He got the name because in childhood he had been a peddler of a kind of Chinese biscuits or dumplings known as po-po.

Another chief, who styled himself a "secretary," was known as Kuo. He and his brother were formerly residents of Shanghai. They had earned a livelihood by writing, to wealthy Chinese, letters demanding money. Failing to get the money, they would throw bombs in at the windows of residences of those addressed. Finally the one brother was arrested by the police in the French concession at

Shanghai, but our chief escaped and turned up as one of the leaders . . . .

The real leader of the bandit gang was a young chap about twenty-five years of age, named Suen Mei-yao. The Suen family was an old and formerly respected family in this district but had been reduced to poverty by the bandits: so, as many others had done, Suen and his father and nephew joined the bandit gang and, because of the standing of the family, became leaders.[3]

J. B. Powell

"Our objects are to protect the poor, bring equality, and slay all immoral officials and gentry."[4]

Sung Fu-chi

'Twas said that the once influential clan of Sun was led by an enlightened man who, falsely charged with banditry, was brought before a corrupt magistrate. Sun's property was confiscated, and his severed head was staked for public scorn. Sun's brother and son swore revenge and fled to the hills.

It was also said that the clan of Sun was itself ruined by bandits, or by idle, gambling sons who squandered the wealth and became associated with salt smugglers. Sun Ming Fu (or was it Sun Mei Tsu?) distinguished himself as a vicious killer, but was slain by the local "volunteer militia." Ever ready to claim merit, the provincial army collected the body, chopped off the head, and posted gruesome photos up and down the railway. Vowing revenge, Sun's brother and son, Kwei-chi and Mei-yao, and their supporters took to the hills where their numbers quickly grew. Discontent was rife, and, after the crops were in, many farmers cast in their lots with that of the outlaws.

In 1898, and again in 1920-1921, the crops were washed away when the Yellow River, called "China's Sorrow," burst its dikes and flooded unimaginably vast areas. During those years, the peasants ate grass, bark if they could find any, and "Goddess of Mercy" soup made from water and the soil that nourished the crops. Sometimes they ate free rice from the government granaries, if the government grandees remembered to free any. Some ate the flesh of the many who grew bloated and died.

As various warlord armies hacked their way across the land, many farmers lost their crops to "taxes," or lost their entire bloodline to conscription or carnage. So it was that bitter bumpkins hoisted their anger into the ancient hills, where some found the reaping of the rifle more palatable than the harvest of the hoe.

Misfits, criminals, and soldiers-of-fortune also sought mountain refuge. Bo-bo or Po-po Liu, onetime peddler of the like-sounding Peking sweet and a "fiend incarnate,"[5] was wanted by the Germans in Tsingtao. Kuo Chi-tsai, one of the chiefs, and his brother had made their Shanghai living by demanding money from their rich countrymen and throwing bombs at anyone who wouldn't pay.[6]

Some of the men were veterans of the Chinese Labor Corps—the 140,000 workers who, between 1916 and 1918, went to France to dig trenches and carry out the menial tasks of the Great War. These coolies were haphazardly educated,

"The bandits looked and behaved like soldiers" 51

and later shipped back and put ashore at Pukow with a few coins in their hands and new ideas in their queueless heads.

Others were graduates of the "university of the forest"[7] but were otherwise illiterate, generally older, and more interested in the devil sweet pipe of opium than in the checkerboard shenanigans of international diplomacy. A few of the ruffians were merely tillers or toilers who had been caught in the heat of a raid and offered a grim choice: join us or die.

The majority of this "Shantung's People's Liberation Society" (alias "The People's Self-Deliverance Army," alias the "National Reconstruction and Autonomy Army"), however, were not from the districts immediately bordering the railway. Many were deserters or "disbanded" soldiers now bound together by old loyalties, by blood oaths and need. Their leadership included foreign and classically educated former army officers.

Sun Mei-yao, among others, had served in the army of a "wild beast"[8] and "a vicious character"[9] named Chang Chin-yao. Chang favored the pro-Japanese Anfus who held Peking through the spring of 1920. When the Chihli army recaptured the capital, Chang's men were routed, but Chang escaped to Japan, leaving his army without funds, "disbanded." Some of the men quickly found mercenary employment elsewhere. Others made the arduous journey back to Shantung or from whence they'd come. But the times were worse than bad, and many men fled to the mountains.

Since the authorities were either unwilling or unable to maintain order in the Lincheng district, emissaries from the wealthy periodically journeyed to the monastery at Pao Tzu Ku bearing "gifts," not for moribund gods but as wise insurance premiums. The outlaws did not scorch the earth like some of the warlords, and the area became an autonomous zone, free of Confucian bureaucrats. It was inhabited by a romantic brotherhood of loafers, dreamers, visionaries, thieves, cutthroats, robbing hoodlums, Robin Hoods, riding through the glen, sacking the odd town or two, and ransoming the gentry or sometimes peons as poor as themselves.

One outlaw band kidnapped a goodly score of their fellow countrymen, partook of hard Chinese bargaining, and made a deal with General Ho Feng-yu. A ransom was paid, immunity was guaranteed and the captives were duly freed. Soon thereafter, forty dripping heads were staked up and down the railway. Thus betrayed, the bandits withdrew into their hideouts, improved their fortifications, stockpiled food and water, and dug in for the winter of 1922.

January, February, March 1923, then two nearby missionary compounds were raided for ransom. Complaints and pressure brought the 20th Army brigade in to clean up the area. With the aid of the fifth and sixth provincial units, they surrounded the bandits' lair at Pao Tzu Ku and demanded its unconditional surrender.

The People's Liberation Society was not inclined to trust its well-being to the mercy of government mercenaries, so the cordon was gradually tightened. By late April, several hundred bandits had been hemmed into their temple stronghold. Realizing that his men were caught in a classical siege, Sun Mei-yao parleyed with neighboring renegade lodges and set up a plan.

On the twenty-first day of the third moon, in the darkness of the hour of the Ox, various coordinated outlaws converged on the railway eight miles south of Lincheng. They captured three policemen who were walking the line.

"The bandits looked and behaved like soldiers" 53

They surrounded and caught two more who were lounging in a foreman's house, seized two railway workers and another guard. The bandits then set upon the rails, tearing out bolts, spikes and fishplates, loosening though not removing eight double lengths of track.

At 2:33 A.M., the largely slumbering Blue Express slipped out of the Shakow station. It chugged along at ten miles per hour until it had cleared two curves, then began an upgrade at twice the pace. Nearly all the passengers were asleep. Nineteen armed guards lounged in a van at the rear of the train. In mufti, their officer was sleeping in another car.

> As the express was approaching kilometer 607 Ganger's house, the engine driver observed on the left side of the track ahead some dark shadows which aroused his suspicions and he decided to apply the brakes. Before he could completely close the brakes, the locomotive gave a sudden jerk. . . .[10]

From their hiding places, the raiders opened up with German Mausers, Japanese rifles, Tsarist-American pieces, anything they had, as the train derailed to a stop. The railway guards scrambled from their van and fired a few feeble rounds, but they were vastly outnumbered and soon melted away as hundreds of howling brigands converged on the crippled train, leisurely demolished it, and then dispersed. Li Ting-yu, Hsu—the Big Nose—and others[11] took their booty and dashed for their respective dens. Sun Mei-yao and his followers, and his allied chiefs and their men, drove their foreign and Chinese captives back into the eastern hills.

Weaving, zigzagging, pausing to rest, then pushing on. Cumbersome, the foreign women were abandoned or sent toward the hounding troops with threatening notes. All hobbled to liberty save Señora Verea, who would not leave her Manuel.

Ling Sun-fu—whose European name was Father William Lenfers—had immediately sent trusted converts into the hills and arranged a meeting. He hiked in many hard miles to a bandit settlement, where he spent the night. In the morning, an armed group marched in and bid the aging priest follow them over the mountain. When they finally reached a temporary headquarters, the mentally agile missionary jockeyed, jollied and bartered for the captives' liberty. Major Robert Allen, Fred Elias—in all six foreigners were supposed to be freed, but another troop train had arrived! Someone was lying, so Father Lenfers got no one; only some letters, a threatening ultimatum, and a guide for the difficult journey back. The guide, however, was a useless rogue who soon abandoned the priest on this, no easy promenade, even for a tough old man-of-God. Then a delightful surprise as Father Lenfers bumped into Dr. Paul Mertons, a Shanghai physician with a clean canteen and a heart good and sturdy enough to make a "house call" on the wealthy and powerful Guiseppe D. Musso, current address: path to the left, path to the right, Shantung mountains. The two men enjoyed a congenial chat, then the priest lumbered on for many li on fragile feet.

Dr. Mertons treated the ailing Musso, then hiked around the settlements and doctored the foreigners one and all. When he prepared to go, the bandits told him to "take her, we don't want her." But Madam Verea would not budge!

"The bandits looked and behaved like soldiers" 55

A train of coolies now weaved its way into this curdled valley bringing, as agreed, rice for the outlaws and canned delights for the foreigners—decent food, even newspapers for a welcome taste of another reality. An outlaw elite also poured over the press, soon lamenting their inadvertent freeing of Lucy T. Aldrich, a chip off the Rock, John D. But the headmen were quite delighted by the depth of the foreign community's anger: the threatened sanctions, the progressive indemnity, the increasing pressure on the Peking Government.

On May 11, Peking gave in and decreed that the siege of Pao Tzu Ku must be lifted. But the bandits had ears and eyes in the hills and at the mines, and the mountains knew nothing of a "troop withdrawal."

On May 14, when Dr. Mertons again hiked in, he was refused permission to treat the hostages. But the foreigners were no longer safely nestled in the valley. Some had been roused in the dark, others in the dawn, and all, by varying footpaths, were again on the move. They fumbled along in a nightmare daydream, deeper into the "Mountains Where The Bandits Live." Down into a glen, up, then down again. A day. A night stumbling into a day—a day with song and scraggly scouts guarding the highest peak yet. Up, up, to a village mustered in celebration. But the foreigners were herded on, higher, through an arbor, and then up steps chiseled in stone. They climbed higher and higher, up through an ancient pailow and into the "Temples Among The Clouds," the "Cloud Nest Shrines"—Chao Yuan Kwan.

Having been made destitute and loneless [homeless?] through incessant civil wars, we are obliged to invite a few foreigners to come up the hill, so that we may make use of them to enforce certain demands and secure certain guarantees, which are, to mention specifically, [1] our readmission into the regular army, and [2] a guarantee for our future safety. We have no intention of ill-treating the foreigners or bringing about diplomatic complications. As money is not our object, it is useless for you to talk to us any more about having them ransomed.[12]

Chapter Six

CLIMB TO THE SUMMIT

"This is really a lovely spot which would be ideal during weekends under different conditions if it were more accessible." [1]

Reginal Rowlatt

"I believe it is the prettiest place I have ever seen in China. ... The various gates and windows of the temples are so arranged, as the Chinese know how, to provide delightful glimpses of some beauty spot on the hill or down in the terraced valley below." [2]

J. B. Powell

"To Whom It May Concern,

Please send a wire to Cheng Cheong, Messrs. Butterfield & Swire, Tientsin: 'Am well. Tell Mother not to worry.'"[3]

Cheng Chi

Five ancient stone dwellings perched on an acre plateau perhaps two-thirds the way up the conical Paotzuku. Impossible cliffs rise two and three hundred feet on three sides, and the front overlooks the ravine and the valley below where, far in the distance, government troops are even now visibly mustering.

Pilgrims, monks, and deities once flourished in these shrines but, though only one building was designed as a stable, all had recently sheltered fragrant donkeys. Two temples still housed centuries old Buddhas, but otherwise the buildings were empty, decaying, here and there partly burned, as if someone had tried arson to purge the sore.

In the arbor a quarter mile down the slope, a constant spring, drinking water—but the outlet was so small that a liter jar emptied it. In the enclosing cliffs and neighboring hills were cracks, fissures, and caves. Perhaps a thousand feet above was the summit, where the guards said the captives would be moved if. . . Bruised and tired from their new round of marches, the twenty-four most valuable hostages now relaxed, contemplated their new surroundings, or reflected on their bizarre lot in life. There were yet some cans of food. Soon a makeshift campfire warmed dinner. Sunset,

Climb to the Summit 59

and a creeping mountain chill. The captives were gathered into the main temple and made to honor the Buddha. Amidst insects, lizards, rodents, and loud smelly keepers, they were forced to bed-down on the earthen floor. In the darkening distance, the coal mine's powerful searchlight began sweeping the countryside.

May 16

In the morning, a queue of outlaw coolies passed near the arched gateway, carrying food and supplies further up the mountain, to the summit they said. Under the lax gaze of a hundred guards, the odd score of hostages was free to roam the compound. Lee Solomon could get around with the aid of a walking stick. Likewise Saphiere, but Hung's feet had given out and he was immobile, as was the ailing Musso, still clad in his Roman nightshirt. The other prisoners lolled about in various "weird costumes."[4] The "irrepressible" old man Smith had "long hair, plenty of whiskers and . . . nothing but a pair of pajamas," blue flannel to be precise. Freddie Elias was sporting "Chinese shoes, Friedman's pants, no shirt, a handkerchief around his neck, straw hat and a coat to fit a fourteen year old boy." Dressed in his own rumpled clothing, J. B. Powell seemed "a tramp with plenty of hair on his face." Big Leon Friedman wore a little suit over his night clothes with "Chinese shoes and cap." Still wearing men's clothing, Señora Verea was holding up well. So was Chi Cheng who wore "coolie clothes"—his Cambridge education and King's English making him a valuable translator. He shared the foreigners' food and treatment, thus faring better than the scores of captured Chinese held in various camps below.

The foreigners called a meeting and organized a "government." Major Roland Pinger was elected "Arbitrator" and "Senior commanding officer." Reginal Rowlatt and Lee Solomon were to serve jointly as "Mayor, Postmaster and Commissary Agents." Friedman took on entertainment, and the gray haired Major Allen, United States Medical Corp, became "Sanitary Inspector." Marcel Berube, a hardy veteran of the Great War who had weathered the marches as so much healthy exercise, was designated the "Official Messenger," and Dr. Siji Hung was declared "Chinese Representative." A room in the stable was set aside as the "mayor's office." The "town council" agreed to assemble every morning, and the captives busied themselves erecting additional fireplaces and cleaning out and occupying the remaining temples.

Far down the valley, a coolie train slowly wound its way toward the sanctuary. When the bearers, more than a dozen, reached the hamlet below, the bandits inspected their load: potatoes, oatmeal, sugar, canned vegetables, bottled "silent" water, cheese, toilet paper, cigars, cigarettes, bandages, candles, books, magazines, newspapers, and other goodies, including a dress for Mrs. Verea, but no guns or contraband so the foreigners got the bulk of it.

Some of the letters the prisoners had written were now appearing in the local English press. Reports of the "success" of the negotiations and the "impending release" of the captives also appeared. According to the bandits, however, no negotiations had yet taken place.

"A very important and busy man," the "Secretary" of the Liberation Society, Chief Kuo, came up from the village to address "his esteemed foreign guests who had come at great trouble and personal sacrifice to help him and his comrades to obtain deliverance from their cruel foes and oppressors—the troops of the Peking Government."[5]

Someone had to go to the coal mines and inform the international community that the government troops had not withdrawn but were actually advancing and that the chiefs were running out of patience. Within the hour, Marcel Berube departed on a "twenty-four hour parole." "The lives of Mr. Powell, Chicago Tribune correspondent, Signor Musso and others were given as a pledge for Berube's return."[6]

The afternoon sun was hot, but the shadows cast by the ancient buildings provided comfort. One temple had a large ornate tablet affixed to the wall. Powell asked one of the Chinese prisoners to translate it.

In stone, in "flowery literary language," the monks had carved an historiette. The temple's founding was obscure, "hidden in the dim dark past." But "in the 16th year of Kang Hsi" (1678) the temple was rebuilt and enjoyed a renaissance, housing three hundred monks and receiving thousands of pilgrims annually. In the 1850s, "the temple was captured by bandits . . . but later delivered by government troops under the local magistrate. After several years, it was retaken by bandits and so on back and forth. . . ."[7]

Powell's thoughts wandered to the "Guatama Buddha in the other world as he looks down on these disciples of his, as the fumes of their opium pipes curl about the battered images erected to his memory." It occured to Powell that "the next tablet will tell of the foreign devils."[8]

After a harangue in the village below, Dr. Mertons was allowed to enter the compound. Commodore Musso was losing weight and quite ill. Several captives had new cuts and bruises, and many were beginning to cough and sneeze, or to complain of stomach trouble, so the good doctor had much to do. During his ministrations, he tactfully sounded out his patients about a possible rescue attempt by foreign troops.

At the village below, renewed celebration: reinforcements had arrived! After several frustrated attempts, three or four hundred Kiangsu rebels under the leadership of Fan Min-hsien had broken through the government lines. Some of them came up to inspect the temples. They were heavily armed and had plenty of ammunition, but wore tattered rags. This apparel was in strong contrast with that of the men who'd sacked the train and now wore colorful, nearly comical combinations of foreign clothes, stolen jewelry, army uniforms, and native garb.

But the renegades were short on food, or else strictly rationing it in case of a long siege. The temple guards seemed to have "skipped lunch," and some of them were quick to lick the hostages' empty cans. Indeed, many were anxious to do small chores in exchange for chow. "Rusky," the coolie who'd been to Siberia, spoke of his Russian wife and children. "Big Lip," so nicknamed because of an injury he'd received from the recoil of his rifle, was a personable chap, and Friedman said there might be a job in his Shanghai garage if. . . . But if nothing else, at least the long marches were, for the moment, over. There were lice to catch and letters to answer as the "Bandit Express" mail service again penetrated the stronghold. Rather than roam the treacherous footpaths in the coming dark, Dr. Mertons shared the captives' food and stayed the night.

Following the Chinese custom, the various temple doors were removed from their hinges and set on the earthen floor as sleeping pallets, but there weren't half enough to go around. Boisterous guards inhabited every building, so the foreigners found little peace. Two chiefs hiked up from the village, and there was an angry ruckus when they discovered some of their sentries playing cards while others slept at their posts. Between the noise, insects, vermin, foul odors, and penetrating cold, a good night's sleep was hard to come by.

May 17

A bath of sorts could be had by heating a little water in "an old fruit can." Washing clothes was likewise no easy matter.

The guards again warned that if the negotiations went poorly, the hostages would be forced to the summit. Dr. Mertons had heard that there might already be hostages there. He and journalist J. B. Powell decided to investigate. Two guards joined their otherwise innocent walk. The foreigners carried a goodly supply of cigarettes and some local Chinese brew.

The climb was steep and rough, so Powell and Mertons rested and gave their escorts a canteen of brandy. "The two worthies gulped it down like so much milk, and within a few minutes both were stretched out on the rock sound asleep."[9]

Another hard hour, and the path abruptly ended at a "gigantic slit" in a sheer vertical wall. But they soon discerned a crude stairway—"hand-holds and wooden pegs driven into the crevices." Here Dr. Mertons demurred. He was exhausted, feared for his heart, and would go no further. J. B., however, pushed on, even though this last two or three hundred feet was like climbing the "Woolworth building."[10] At the crest, he found "a huge unguarded wooden door."

The area was flat, pear-shaped, about two acres. A line of fortified trenches and dugouts circled the outer perimeter, and all around was a haunting view of the rugged Shantung "Robber Mountains."

Suddenly a sentry, but Powell offered his canteen and tobacco. The man mellowed, indulged himself, volunteered a tour.

A second line of trenches protected the inner core. Scattered here and there were large jugs for catching rainwater, and someone had laboriously carved three huge cisterns into the chilling rock. In and out of a hut crammed with flour, bean cake, and other fragrant delights, but a foul odor came from one shack. Powell drew aside a matted curtain and stepped into a fetid room "filled to suffocation with Chinese children."[11] Toddlers to teenagers, they were filthy, scabby, and listless on their straw beds. "Most of them were in rags, the few that were still clinging to their bodies being silk and satin, mute testimonial to the standing of their families."[12]

Having seen his fill, Powell plied the guard with more tobacco, then retraced his steps down the skyscraper. He informed Dr. Mertons of his grisly findings, they awoke their snoozing guards and returned to the temple compound.

Another coolie train loaded with goodies had reached the temples. This boxed treasure had been deposited at the "mayor's office," where the contents were being checked against an invoice to discourage theft. Along with a wide variety of compact foods and welcome reading matter, there were medicine, blankets, tins of sterno, and other practical equipment for the comfort of captive campers.

Dr. Mertons again practiced his healing arts, then made ready to leave. Several captives gave him letters, and Reginal Rowlatt, who'd somehow kept twenty-five dollars safely hidden from his captors, now entrusted this money to the doctor's safe keeping.

Through the arch of honor, down the stairs, through the arbor, and into the bandit camp, where Mertons was treated to another harangue about the government's lies. Then he began in earnest the hard, hilly hike back to the coal mines at Tsaochuang.

After several hours, Mertons encountered a large party of Chinese government officials en route to the stronghold. The bigwigs were carried in sedan chairs. Sundry scribes rode donkeys, and half a dozen relief coolies walked.

Escorted in by a motley "guard of honor," this delegation reached the bandit village at 2:30 P.M. and almost immediately joined the outlaw headmen in one of the larger shacks. This "mud-hut conference" dragged on, deep into the night, into the dawn, and well into the morning before the government team left, having concluded nothing. Sometime before midnight, however, captive Chen Shih-ying, a former district salt inspector who had been traveling to Peking to complete a cure, died, "partly from exposure and chiefly from lack of food."[13]

May 18

After the negotiators were safely away, the government troops again pressed the bandit lines. As the day wore on, there was intermittent firing, and a couple of outlaws were killed or wounded by marksmen. The prison plateau became tense; the guards less kind.

As day drew toward evening, the chiefs again gathered and argued strategy. Their discussions were sometimes fiery and ominous, as when old Bo-bo Liu demanded that they kill a couple of foreigners to convince the government they meant business. When a consensus was hammered out, several outlaws hiked up to the temples, called the hostages together, and announced their intentions. Marcel Berube would take a message—this time to Peking! If the government troops were not withdrawn in four days, one American and one Britisher would be shot!

A charged silence, then one, several more, and finally most of the hostages broke forth in a hopeful, prayerful, defiant, and, to the outlaws, totally incomprehensible song.

Coal black and overcast. Riding a pony that sometimes lost its footing and stumbled, Marcel Berube followed the sounds of his guide, for, although the man was only a few yards ahead, he was "quite invisible." But the night was too dark, the path too pitched, and, as urgent as their mission was, they had to halt in a hamlet and wait for dawn.

May 19

Government men were again chaired into the bandit nest. They carried signed and sealed army commissions and a plan. But the outlaws weren't impressed with the proffered parchments and now ordered several hostages to be imprisoned on the summit. One of the chiefs hiked up to the compound and selected Lee Solomon and Majors Pinger and Allen. Americans all, they began packing their meager possessions.

The foreign men now spoke up and prevailed upon Señor Verea to convince his wife to leave with the Chinese delegation—to get out while she still could, and the Vereas finally agreed. One of the government men surrendered his palanquin, and at about 7:00 P.M., Señora Verea bid goodbye to her Manuel and the men with whom she'd shared a harrowing fortnight. After threatening all day, rain began to fall.

> In a very few minutes the path was slippery, and the bearers who carried Mrs. Verea . . . were hardly able to keep their feet on the treacherous surface. As the night wore on, the rain fell faster and faster, and the intense darkness added to the danger. One hill alone took nearly two hours to cross, the bearers slipping and sliding in the mud on the mountain path. Once, exhausted by the struggle, the coolies declared that they could go no farther, but General Ting, with threats and promises, persuaded them to renew their battle against the elements. It was after two a.m. when the sorely tried party trailed slowly into Tsaochuang. The camp was instantly awake. . . .[14]

It is all a nightmare too terrible for words. They took me away from my husband at first but when I begged to remain with him they allowed me to do so. His hair has gone white and he was on the verge of collapse. We were separated from the others after the first night, then forced to march day after day, sometimes all night. . . . On the second day, a Chinese ahead of me slipped and fell over the cliff.

In the hill camp we were alone but never had any privacy. The bandits caroused, drank and smoked opium. The first week, we were fed twice daily but were too afraid to eat. Then when the food from the U.S. Rescue Mission came, it was like manna from Heaven. The courage of the foreigners was splendid. They tried to make light of the most perilous times and smile.

I was several times offered my liberty, but how could I leave my husband when a bride?

On Friday some bandits were killed and others wounded by sharpshooters. They were terribly angry and threatened reprisals if the firing continued. After the parleys with the Government envoys, the bandit chiefs were furious. They ordered the Americans to the Summit of Paotzekou and ordered the others to follow today. Then the foreigners urged my husband to make me return and gave me great cheers as we said good-bye. But I am desolate. Please ask all foreigners in China to insist on the release of their companions in Paozekou before it is too late.[15]

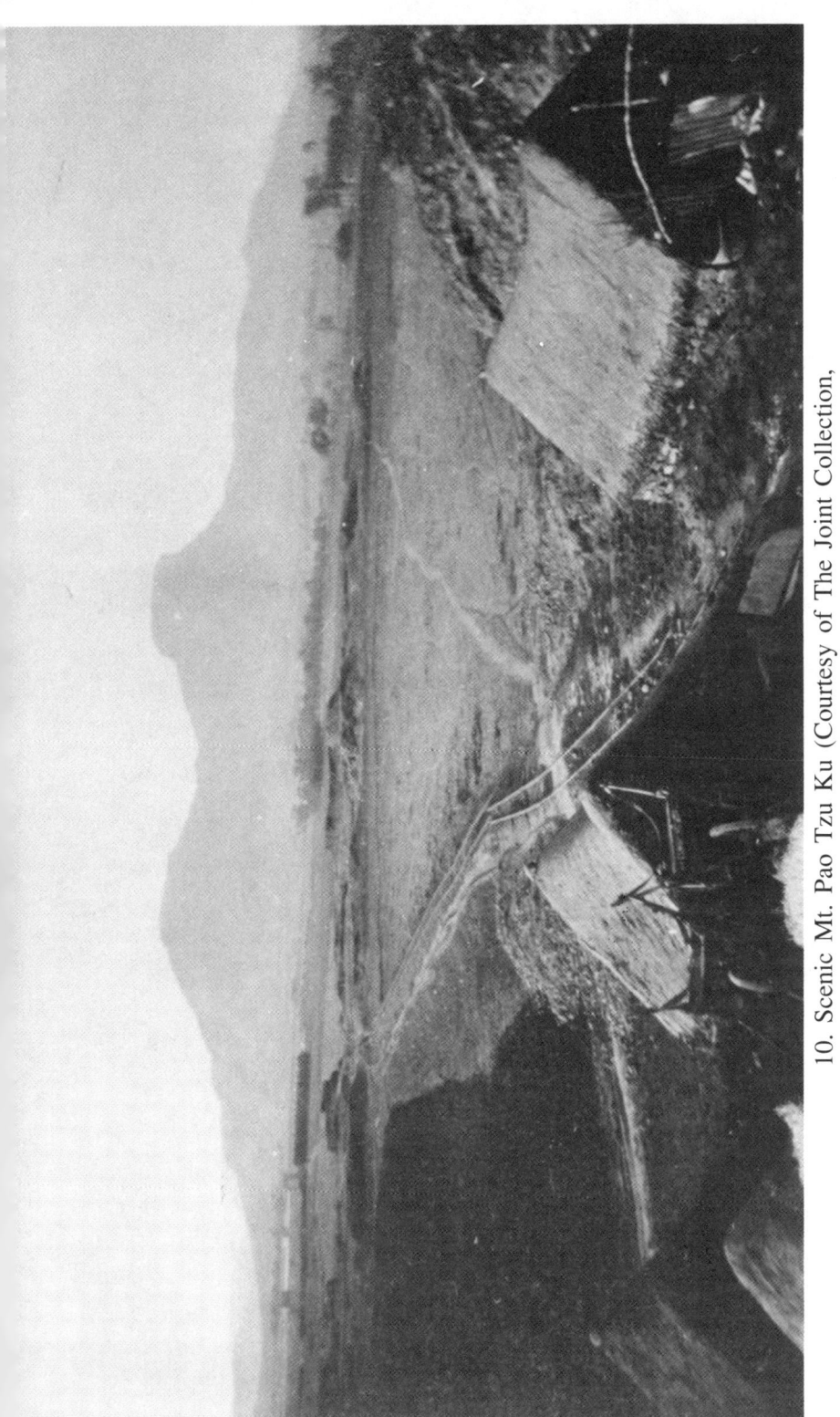

10. Scenic Mt. Pao Tzu Ku (Courtesy of The Joint Collection, University of Missouri).

11. Jerome Henley "on parole" at the mines (Courtesy of The Joint Collection, University of Missouri).

12. Marcel Berube poses with two native bearers (Courtesy of The Joint Collection, University of Missouri).

13. The bandit "secretary" Kuo Chi-tsai (Courtesy of The Illustrated London News Picture Library).

14. Major Roland Pinger near the entrance to the "Sap Club" (Courtesy of The Illustrated London News Picture Library).

15. At the Temple stronghold: Cheng Chi, center, Lee Solomon in profile, and various outlaws (Courtesy of The Joint Collection, University of Missouri).

16. Roy Anderson, an American born in China of missionary parents, en route into the bandit's stronghold (Courtesy of The Joint Collection, University of Missouri).

17. Lee Solomon and J. B. Powell (Courtesy of The Joint Collection, University of Missouri).

18. Russian cartoonist's view of the "motley People's Self-Deliverance Army". (Illustration by Ricardo Guerrero Jr.).

Chapter Seven

NEGOTIATIONS

One of the principal difficulties at Lincheng at present is the inability to get the telegraphic messages away promptly. There is only one old and very slow operator at this small station, and though he works 22 out of the 24 hours, he is utterly unable to cope with the flood of telegrams, many of which are in code.[1]

The Peking and Tientsin Times

70   *Outrage at Lincheng*

My whole time since the morning of May 6th had been occupied in coding and decoding telegrams, meeting trains from the south and taking released and escaped captives to the hospital, sending foreign doctors and medical supplies to the scene of the holdup, and keeping in communication with the Military Governor's office. During sixty-five hours, I had had but four hours sleep[2]

H. L. Milbourne
American Vice-Consul, Tsinan-fu

May 6

Through the efforts of Paul P. Whitham of Asia Development, the American consulate at Tsinan was quickly alerted to the attack, but official confirmation proved impossible. Telephone service was minimal, limited to a few cities. The railway authorities knew nothing, and Shantung's civil and military governors' offices had no information.[3] Shortly before midnight, Naill and Weisenberg's first telegrams came in, and Schurman alerted Washington.

May 7

Born in Rumania, Joseph Rothman, the Britisher killed on the train, had spent the early part of his life in South Africa where he fought the Dutch during the Boer War. In

1902 in Cape Colony, he became a naturalized British subject, but he was a vagabond, a sharpy, and later surfaced as a Shanghai wheeler-dealer. Rothman had only recently returned to China after an extended stay in Manila. Low on cash, he may have been traveling north in search of work. His body was taken to the platform at Lincheng where, leaving no known relatives, it marinated.

At 7:00 A.M., Dr. Schurman and other dignitaries left Tsinan for a now abbreviated inspection of some repair work on the Yellow River dike. Meanwhile, consul Milbourne and a British colleague visited the military governor and demanded immediate action. When Milbourne returned to the consulate, there were two more telegrams from Naill and Weisenberg:

> Situation unchanged. Military getting no results. Am trying to communicate with captives. Rumor foreigners placed in front of bandits. Military can't fire. Report another foreigner killed.

> Miss McFadden and Miss Coralti released. Am sending to Tsinan. Soldiers must withdraw immediately or bandits will kill all foreigners. Report two Americans killed, one British dying. Doctor urgently needed. Powell sick still held by bandits.[4]

Milbourne phoned the military governor's office and "demanded a special train to send foreign doctors and medical supplies to the scene."[5] Then he called the Christian University Hospital and "requested that two foreign and two Chinese doctors and adequate medical supplies be in readiness."[6] He chauffeured the doctors to the railway, saw them aboard the slowly assembled train, and returned to the government compound, to find two more telegrams.

> Four more women released. All very ill. Names will follow. Have doctors meet train. One American shot. Bandits surrounded. Continuous firing. Foreigners in grave danger.
>
> American authorities must act immediately. Miss Aldrich, Senator's daughter, very ill. Two Americans reported shot. . . .[7]

Milbourne went right back to the depot and waited for the long delayed train. Miss Coralti, Thomas Day and M. C. Jacobsen arrived in good spirits, but Misses McFadden and Schonberg "had to be bodily carried from the train."[8] Milbourne drove them to the hospital, then returned to the consulate and was soon in conference with a member of the military governor's staff.

Señor J. Bathalha De Freitas, Envoy Extraordinary and Minister Plentipotentiary of the Republic of Portugal and doyen ("dean") of the Peking Diplomatic Corps, spent most of the day out of town. When he returned, he met with Sir Ronald Macleay—Britain's Envoy Extraordinary—Counsellor Edward Bell of the American Legation, and the Italian minister. The men agreed: the first priority of the Chinese government must be the release of the hostages, that the Chinese authorities must not endanger the captives with military operations, and that any ransom must be borne by the Chinese. Since the French ambassador was already at Paoting-fu for discussions with Tsao Kun, they telegraphed him to press the Lincheng matter personally. In the predawn hours, Naill and Weisenberg withdrew their report that two Americans had been killed.

May 8

Throughout China, the foreign press gave front page coverage to the Lincheng kidnappings, but "the initial news reports proved to be very unreliable."[9] One or two Americans had not been killed; no Britisher was dying. Major Pinger, who was reported both as killed and as wounded, was actually only limping from the strain of the marches. These errors were soon compounded because, in lieu of an effective wire-service, the various small newspapers reprinted paraphrased versions of each other's mistakes.

At 1:00 P.M., Doyen De Freitas met with Premier Chang, delivered a formal protest, and "further requested that any sort of military operations against the bandits should be suspended."[10]

> The Premier, who appeared to be much moved, said that he was doing his best to save the foreigners and he deeply regretted the incident. . . .
>
> The Minister of Communications told the dean that the first consideration of the government is the freedom of the foreign captives, and after this had been accomplished, the military governors of Kiangsu, Anhui and Shantung will be instructed to round up the bandits with a view of punishing them. . . .[11]

De Freitas rejoined his foreign colleagues. After discussion, it was decided that in addition to any material damages claimed, a progressive indemnity would be demanded if the hostages were not freed within four days. The British Ambassador suggested that the only way to render the Tientsin-Pukow railway safe might be to place it under foreign management.

May 9

Harvey Milbourne got a call from the military governor's office informing him that Generals Wu Chang Chi and Ho Feng-yu were to consult with Mr. Naill for the release of the foreign captives and asking him to relay the message.[12] Milbourne did so immediately; it was 1:00 A.M. By 11:00 A.M., Milbourne and the British consul were back at the governor's office keeping the pressure on.

Sir Ronald Macleay, in a rare personal visit to the Chinese Foreign Ministry, characterized the affair as "one of the most serious incidents which had arisen between China and the Powers since the events of 1900"[13]—when the Boxer madness was upon the land!

May 10

A trickle of protests now reached the various legations in Peking and the home offices in London and Washington.

As various clubs and organizations met in emergency sessions, this trickle grew into a deluge of telegraphic outrage. Consul Milbourne suffered some frustration of his own.

> For some unexplained reason, the two British doctors whom I had sent to Lincheng on May 7th, returned to Tsinan; one on May 9th, and the other on May 10th. Almost immediately after the second doctor had left Lincheng, I received telegrams from Consul Davis at Lincheng and from Mr. Naill at Tsaochuang requesting me to send an American doctor. Again after considerable difficulty, I secured a special train and sent Dr. Heimburger, an American from Shantung Christian University.[14]

May 11

The growing rescue operation was centering at the twenty-five acre Chung Hsing coal mines at Tsaochuang. Entirely surrounded by a huge, machine-gun equipped, electrified wall, this massive compound was being inundated with diplomats, reporters, and military men. The French and Italian consuls from Shanghai had reached the wreck early. Various Americans made their way later. Although none of his nationals was missing, a Japanese representative showed up. May 8, 9, and 10 saw additional Chinese troops converging on the scene, although supplies arrived slower than men. Dozens of friends and relatives of the captives came, some seeking a private deal with the outlaws. Several doctors were summoned, but no one had to call out the vendors and the curiosity and thrill seekers who likewise converged on the coal mines at Tsaochuang. Since there were no western-style hotels in the neighborhood, the T-P Railway moved an increasing number of Blue sleeping and dining cars onto the siding inside the fortress. Nearly overnight, an international railway boomtown sprang into being.

May 12

The United Services Association—British veterans of the Great War—held a packed Extraordinary General Meeting at the Gordon Hall in Tientsin. Brother Rowlatt was missing! The angry gathering unanimously forwarded a resolution to Sir Ronald Macleay assuring him of their "unqualified support in any steps, however drastic. . . ."

May 13

The Legation at Peking to the Secretary of State

On early morning 13th a band of men, possibly soldiers, attempted to rob a bank in Tangshan. General fright ensued and, as it was feared an attempt might be made to loot railway property, the company of American troops stationed there prepared for action, but fortunately no necessity arose.[15]

A settlement seemed near. The outlaws' terms were known, Shantung's military governor had agreed, and Roy Anderson and S. T. Wen had again journeyed into the hills in hopes of completing an agreement.

May 14

Chinese Foreign Office state they expect negotiations will soon be completed for prisoners' release.

At meeting of the diplomatic body today it was decided that the dean should remind the Foreign Office that the requested indemnity had been running since May 12, 12 p.m. It has not yet been definitely settled whether this progressive indemnity shall be in cash or in the nature of "sanctions," that is, undertakings for proper policing and control of railways in the future.[16]

In the dark, inexplicably, the outlaws broke camp and drove their hostages deeper into the "Mountains Where the Bandits Live."

Tsaochuang, May 15

The optimism which has been prevailing for the last few days regarding the release of the prisoners has unfortunately proved premature. A settlement seems as far off as ever.[17]

May 16

Anger and exasperation dominated the morning meeting of the Diplomatic Corps, and the ministers plentipotentiary decided to consult with their admirals and governments about a possible naval demonstration "to remind the people of

China that there is a point beyond which we cannot be flouted."[18]

A delegation of outlaws now emerged from their hills and entered the fortified colliery. They came to reconnoiter the situation, but also to invite Anderson and Wen to visit them in their stronghold the following day. The bandits did a bit of shopping, slipped Carl Crow four gold watches they'd overwound, broken, and wanted repaired, and returned to their lair.

May 17

Wen and Anderson had hoped to meet again with the outlaw chiefs, but their plan was thwarted by Peking's minister of communications and Tientsin's chief of Police who, at 6:00 A.M., sent an advance party to the robbers.[19] Until this delegation returned, the multitude of officials gathered at the mines could do little more than dispatch supplies.

Between May 10 and 17, the American Minister, Dr. Schurman, was in Shanghai on a tour arranged prior to the train wreck.[20] Anxious over the delay in the release of the captives and wanting to discuss the proposed naval demonstration with his colleagues, Dr. Schurman cut short his trip and headed north along the same route as the Blue Express.[21] At Lincheng—a scheduled halt.

Consul Davis and Major Philoon boarded the minister's special train and briefed Schurman on the latest. They suggested that the recent delays had been due to the "great difficulties experienced in arriving at a plan acceptable to all bandit chiefs."[22] Davis and Philoon were also apprehensive that the situation could be complicated by the number of Chinese officials involved. Schurman reached Peking in the morning and prepared a report for the State Department wherein, for the moment, he advised against naval maneuvers.

May 19

Disturbing news from Consul Davis at Tsaochuang.

> Banditti released Berube this morning to bring letters to consuls stating that, the troops are now within one or two miles of Paotzuku and that, unless withdrawn immediately, fighting must ensue in which safety of foreign prisoners cannot be guaranteed.[23]

Now evidently quite exasperated by the profusion of officials, dignitaries, and military men hanging about, Consul Davis closed by saying, "Suggest diplomatic body ascertain and inform us who is Chinese head here."[24]

> The Diplomatic Body urgently remind the Chinese Government of the assurances given them that the withdrawal of these troops was to be effected immediately, and, in order to safeguard the lives of the captives, insist that this belated action be taken forthwith, and that to this end a telegram be addressed in their name to Marshal Tsao Kun in his capacity of Inspector-General of the provinces of Chihli, Shantung, and Honan. . . .[25]

Bearing sealed army commissions for the bandit leadership, General Ting and company were again chaired into the mountains. But their parchments were refused, and they were sent away with the reluctantly freed Mrs. Verea. A torrential downpour turned the tricky footpaths into grabbing slime.

It was after 2:00 A.M. when the drenched delegation reached the mines. The camp was instantly awake, but the gaiety was quickly shattered by Señora Verea's news that there was fighting and that several Americans had been forced to the summit.

In the 5:00 A.M. darkness, Davis and Philoon telegraphed these developments to Dr. Schurman and concluded:

> We believe further negotiations withholding foreign representation futile. Anderson willing to go provided Chinese Government gives plentipotentiary powers. Otherwise direct foreign negotiations only hope early release. . . . The situation very serious.[26]

Dr. Schurman didn't object to Anderson continuing the negotiations provided the bandits understand that he spoke for the Chinese only and not in any way for the American government. Schurman also informed Washington that "the outlook is worse than it has been. The possibility of shooting and the probability of delay in negotiations must be recognized."[27]

Chapter Eight

EARLY NAVAL BARBARIANS

The Chinese, a tremendously durable people, possess the largest country and longest civilization known to mankind. They have uninterruptedly existed as a political and cultural entity for well over 4000 years, a record no country in the world can match. The Chinese were old when ancient Greece was young; they produced Confucius centuries before Alexander the Great or Julius Caesar; they were having a magnificently mature development when Europe was a medieval shambles. Chinese history goes back at least to 2800 B.C. The birth of Solomon, the death of Socrates, the birth of Jesus, the death of Charlemagne, the birth of Newton, the death of Bismarck, all took place while China was *the same nation. We do not know the origins of the Chinese. They have always been there. They seem older than the rocks.*[1]

John Gunther

In A.D. 635 . . . the ruling T'ang emperor issued this decree:

> The Way has more than one name. There is more than one Sage. Doctrines vary in different lands, but their benefits reach all mankind. A man of great virtue has brought books and images from afar to present them in our capital. After examining his doctrines, we find them profound and pacific. This religion does good to all men. Let it be preached freely in the empire.

It is believed that the "man of virtue" was named Reuben. The doctrine he brought for the first time to China was certainly Christianity.[2]

The Chinese Looking Glass

Chinese soil spawned Taoism and Confucianism, but the Buddhism that flourished there was carried across the mountains from India. Zoroastrianism also found its way to the Middle Kingdom, as did the forever wandering Jews. Moslem Arabs came; some stayed, others traded and carried China's endless inventions far into the several seas. The Flowery Kingdom was a civilized oasis in an otherwise barbarian orb, and many distant peoples heard of her wisdom, wealth and achievements and sent tribute-laden emissaries to view the splendor, learn from it, and emerge richer for having touched it.

In the seventh Christian century, when the heretical Nestorians sought freedom of worship, they were not denied nor forced to accept Buddhism or Taoism. Many Buddhists were also Taoists. Many Taoists were also Buddhists, and both knew the teachings of Confucius and had probably learned something from the Jews or Arabs or dozens of other sects or minorities. Having touched many "truths," the Chinese were generally eclectic in their religious tastes so that a new way, a Christian way, could be allowed to add its truth to the greater cup of wisdom.

Sitting in contemplative repose in one Cantonese temple are "five hundred life-size images of gilded wood, representing deified sages of the Buddhist faith."[3] One of these minor gods, a guardian of travelers, seems a bit peculiar in his thirteenth century Florentine regalia—Polo, Marco.

An enterprising merchant, Marco Polo ventured into the kingdom when the conquering Mongols were still consolidating their power. Ghenghis Khan had been so murderously destructive that they couldn't trust many Chinese to help them administer the shattered mess. The great Khan's grandson, Kublai Khan, thus found talent where he could. He hired some Arabs and gave Polo a job as a mandarin. Marco loyally served his mentor for twenty years before returning to Italy.

In 1294, the Kublai Khan died, and for the next forty years, seven different men ruled more by butchery than benevolence. After a Chinese rebellion, with devastation lasting a generation, the Mongols were expelled through the Great Wall, and an unschooled peasant and former monk became the emperor of a new Ming Dynasty.

For fourteen years, the robust Ming rebuilt Peking into an architectural dream and then moved the capital there from Nanking. The Grand Canal was likewise improved to insure a steady flow of southern grain. Annam, modern day Vietnam, was reoccupied and for twenty years again made a Chinese province. As word of the Ming vitality spread, many foreign emissaries journeyed to Peking, bringing exotic tribute and trinkets.

In 1514, naval barbarians hit China's shores. Forewarned by the traveled Arabs that these hairy, unwashed people were vagabond pirates, the Chinese kept a vigilant eye. An official embassy from the "King of Portugal" to the "King of China" soon reached Canton.[4] Bearing gifts for the emperor, Tomé Pires was allowed to proceed to Peking via the slow, inland canal route. But four other, unofficial Portuguese ships sailed up the Pearl River and "almost at once started launching bloody little forays along its banks, looting and slaughtering until the Chinese viceroy was obliged to mount a military operation against them."[5] This piracy, plus a complaint from the King of Malacca, wrecked the Pires mission.

In 1520-1521, Pires tried again, but the Chinese and Portuguese had met in a naval conflict, Pires was thrown into prison, where he died, and the Chinese expelled the Portuguese from Canton. But these hardy Europeans kept coming. In the 1540s, they constructed a fort near Ningpo "and once more began robbing, killing, and behaving like marauding gangs of freebooters."[6] Again they were thrown out. Around

1557, the ever-patient Chinese finally confined the Portuguese to Macao and walled off the peninsula to avoid contamination.

But still more buccaneers came. By mid-century, Japanese cutthroats were plundering the Chinese coast, and "these sporadic raids escalated into full-fledged invasions in which Chinese local bandits and off-shore pirates joined forces with the Japanese."[7] In time, the tiring Ming mustered enough troops to restore tranquility.

At Macao, a more subtle invasion was under way. Matteo Ricci and others shed their Catholic robes, donned the Confucian scholar's gown, studied the Chinese classics, and sought out native intellectuals for some learned chit-chat. A decade of cultivation paid off when Ricci was invited to spend two months in the capital.

But the 1590s hadn't gone well for the Chinese. In 1592, the Japanese overran Korea, with Peking in their sights. The Chinese eventually reconquered their "vassal kingdom," but this hollow victory utterly drained the treasury. At this point, the Dutch reached Canton, and the British were close behind.

The Emperor Wan-li did not trouble himself with these new ruffians or with the nation's weakened monetary structure or loss of prestige. Instead, he regularly swept peasants off their land so that imperial friends and family might amass vast estates. He dedicated himself to "drinking, opium smoking, philandering, squandering the state funds and ordering harsh punishment to all opposition."[8] The mountains soon held many angry men.

Wan-li took little notice of such trivialities. He was, however, intrigued with two clocks and a clavichord that

Matteo Ricci presented at court. As a reward, Ricci was allowed to remain in Peking as a visiting scholar, even though, as one Chinese official cautioned, "Where he comes from it is impossible to say, the alleged name of his country being untraceable in our records."[9]

To explain where Rome and Portugal were located, Ricci prepared a map of the world, but as Father Trigault recorded, the Chinese did not "like the idea of our geographies pushing their China into one corner of the Orient...." Ricci, therefore, "left a margin on either side of the map, making the Kingdom of China appear right in the centre. This was more in keeping with their ideas and gave them a great deal of pleasure and satisfaction."[10]

The erudite mandarins may have been pleased, but the peons were not. Armed, hungry men were coming down from their hills, roaming, robbing, and looting the countryside. Along the walled northern frontier, the Manchus were grabbing up parcels of land and administering them so well that many Ming officials changed loyalties. Meanwhile, a new emperor ascended the Dragon Throne. His chief interest was not debauchery. Instead, he devoted himself to carpentry. Not an ignoble calling, but much like playing the *chin* or violin while the empire crumbled.

To combat the increasing lawlessness, the Ming Court sought Portuguese and Jesuit help in securing cannon. The Christians delivered, but it was too little too late. The rebels defeated several Ming armies and captured Peking. The emperor hanged himself and, in desperation, a Ming general invited the Manchus in through the Great Wall to crush the peasants. Manchu bannermen indeed routed the peasants, but then they wouldn't leave. Instead, in 1644, the Manchus proclaimed the dynasty known as Ch'ing.

Among other curiosities the Manchus found in Peking was a small, highly trained Jesuit community. Adam Schall, who'd earlier cast twenty large cannons for the Ming, was now peaceably revising the calendar. His efforts were not disturbed. Indeed, the first Manchu emperor became "very friendly toward Schall and sometimes sought the aged missionary's advice."[11]

In 1662, K'ang-hsi received the Mandate of Heaven, and he wisely administered the Celestial Empire for sixty years. But not without problems. Russian and Chinese troops clashed in the far north, but with the aid of two Jesuits, a peace treaty settled the disputed boundaries. Pleased with the missionaries' performance, K'ang-hsi "issued an edict of toleration for the Christian religion in China," and "these events inaugurated the most successful two decades of the Jesuit mission."[12]

In 1722, when K'ang-hsi died, the problem of succession plagued the Imperial House as more than one relative sought the throne. Yung-cheng won the struggle, but brought with him a grudge against the missionaries, some of whom had sided against him. In 1724, the emperor declared Christianity a subversive organization and ordered the persecution of Christians everywhere in the kingdom except at Court.

Like his grandfather, Ch'ien-lung would reign for more than sixty years and "had the good fortune to rule a nation at peace during the height of its dynastic power."[13] The treasury was full, and crop yields kept pace with the increasing population. The Emperor of the World therefore had the leisure to pen some forty thousand poems, and to sponsor a variety of cultural endeavors, such as the renovation and expansion of the old Summer Palace—including a miniature Versailles designed in the Italian style by Jesuit architects.

The empire continued tranquil. There was a bit of trouble with some frontier peoples, but their suppression provided the Manchu generals with a means of amassing illicit fortunes. The European "Men of the Western Ocean" were now content to trade exclusively at Canton on Chinese terms, but the Chinese officials didn't take much interest in this barter. They allowed it to help civilize the nomads, although the benevolence the Celestial Court was willing to bestow had its limits. In 1793, the Earl of Macartney came to Peking seeking formal diplomatic relations and additional ports-of-entry for British ships. The Earl was received courteously, but the epistles the Emperor Ch'ien-lung sent to George III were less than encouraging.

An Imperial Edict to the King of England

You, O King, are so inclined toward our civilization that you have sent a special envoy across the seas to bring to our Court your memorial of congratulations on the occasion of my birthday and to present your native products as an expression of your thoughtfulness. On perusing your memorial, so simply worded and sincerely conceived, I am impressed by your genuine respectfulness and friendliness and greatly pleased.

As to the request made in your memorial, O King, to send one of your nationals to stay at the Celestial Court to take care of your country's trade with China, this is not in harmony with the state system of our dynasty and will definitely not be permitted. . . .[14]

Early Naval Barbarians 89

A further mandate clarified just what boons the Chinese emperor would grant.

> Your Ambassador requests facilities for ships of your nation to call at Ningpo, Chusan, Tientsin and other places for purposes of trade . . . . For the future, as in the past, I decree that your request is refused.
> The request that your merchants may establish a repository in the capital of my Empire for the storing and sale of your produce. . . . This request is also refused.
> Your request for a small island near Chusan where your merchants may reside and goods be warehoused . . . cannot possibly be entertained.
> The next request, for a small site in the vicinity of Canton city where your merchants may lodge . . . is contrary to precedent. . . . From every point of view, therefore, it is best that the regulations now in force should continue unchanged. . . .
> If, after the receipt of this explicit decree, you lightly give ear to the representations of your subordinates and allow your barbarian merchants to proceed to Chekiang and Tientsin, with the object of landing and trading there, the ordinances of my Celestial Empire are strict in the extreme, and the local officials, both civil and military, are bound reverently to obey the law of the land. Should your vassals touch the shore, your merchants will assuredly never be permitted to land or to reside there, but will be subject to instant expulsion. In that event your barbarian merchants will have had a long journey for nothing. Do not say that you were not warned in due time! Tremblingly obey and show no negligence! A special mandate![15]

It is doubtful that King George III "trembled," but Great Britain did not dispatch another official expedition until 1816. Even then, Lord Amherst fared no better.

> We accept your tribute and to acknowledge your devotion have in turn conferred presents. However, your presents are of no interest or use. In future do not bother to dispatch them, for they are merely a waste of time. If you loyally accept Our Sovereignty, there is no need for these state appearances to prove that you are indeed our vassal.[16]

Rapidly colonizing the setting sun, Great Britain would soon prove irresistible, but for one more generation, China's worst problems would lay within.

The Yellow River, called "China's Sorrow," repeatedly overflowed during the first decades of the nineteenth century. Each flood brought gargantuan devastation, and the countless silver taels earmarked for dike-repair moved instead into the purses of leeching magistrates. The Grand Canal filled with silt and provided a second easy route to dirty money. The government Salt Monopoly festered with corruption. Land taxes became brutally arbitrary and fell most heavily on the poor, and "government services" progressively served only the elitist scholarcrats administering them. Meanwhile, millions of peasants dined on elaborate tables of nothingness, and mud. More and more mud. Foreign mud. Opium.

The various prohibitions were repeated, but opium's profits were huge, pushers plentiful, and addicts progressively more abundant. Common in the lower levels of the bureaucracy, but drug addiction fouled peasant and palace alike. A mire of mud ruining China's "balance of payments." Mud paid for in silver and souls.

By the 1830s, the importation of opium and the outflow of ingots reached a dimension where even dreamy Peking could no longer feign ignorance. Thus, in 1839, the emperor sent Commissioner Lin to Canton to destroy this fetid trade.

In his wisdom, Lin decreed a period of grace during which the foreigners could surrender their stocks and quit their evil ways without penalty. After that, Celestial Justice would provide death to growers, death to dealers, death to users, and death to the barbarians who shipped the drugs ashore!

Having heard all this before, the multinational merchants paid little heed. Commissioner Lin responded by blockading them into their "factories." After six lonely weeks, having no ready alternatives, the foreigners surrendered some twenty-five hundred addictive tons.

Realizing that this huge haul was still only part of one year's shipments, Lin pressed the problem internationally.

> Let us ask, where is your conscience? I have heard that the smoking of opium is very strictly forbidden by your country; that is because the harm caused by opium is clearly understood. Since it is not permitted to do harm to your own country, then even less should you let it be passed on to the harm of other countries—how much less to China! Of all that China exports to foreign countries, there is not a single thing which is not beneficial to people: they are of benefit when eaten, or of benefit when used, or of benefit when resold: all are beneficial. Is there a single article from China which has done any harm to foreign countries?[17]

This, and a great deal more, Lin eloquently penned to Victoria Ying-kuo wang, the "Ruler of England." Nevertheless, within three years, the modern British war-machine had destroyed China's medieval forces, and the Manchu Dynasty had capitulated.[18] Four more ports were forced open to "free trade" and expensive poppy.

Lin Tse-hsu had learned much about the barbarians' thoughts and technology, and he continued to warn about the danger they presented. But Lin had been dismissed and exiled, so he no longer wrote to the emperor but to his friends, and he was obliged to beg that his opinions be kept secret.

But the foreigners' immediate impact continued small—five coastal cities and the rivers that nourished them. The great inland subcontinent was superficially unscathed, so, while smugly basking in their manifestly self-evident cultural superiority, most Chinese scholar-officials made little effort to comprehend these pugnacious seaborne barbarians. Until the 1860s, China's "foreign policy" was simply to ignore, or at best to silently obstruct, the European onslaught.

The Flowery Kingdom had long exported silks, teas, and bric-a-brac. Now, as living conditions became abominable, cheap labor coolies were added to the invoice. Many died on the slave ships. But the many more who stayed at home fared little better. Hundreds of thousands died of starvation. Millions perished in the Nien, Moslem, or Miao rebellions or when Hung Hsiu-ch'uan lost his head to a warped vision.

Hung told his followers that he was Jesus Christ's younger brother and that God Almighty had given him the sacred duty of driving the alien Manchus through the Wall. Between 1850 and 1864, the Celestial Dynasty and Hung's Heavenly Kingdom of Great Peace fought in one of the bloodiest conflagrations in planetary history. The Manchus—with a hardy helping of Chinese support, plus some foreign arms and mercenaries—finally "won," which is to say that they ruled the ruins.

The countryside was devastated. An Imperial Renaissance took place as the new leadership cleared the rubble, instituted reforms, fostered reconstruction, and finally turned a conservative eye toward the Western problem.

European death technology had again proven superior, so China sought to purchase and manufacture these weapons. The empire at long last established a foreign affairs department. The slogan of the day became "self-strengthening," or as Wei Yuan had advised an unheeded generation earlier, "Learn the superior skills of the barbarians in order to control them."[19] But the urgency of the foreigners' threat again diminished, and the majority of China's educated elite once again turned their pens and pipes to the contemplation of previous scholars' commentaries on certain obscure passages in the ancient Confucian texts examining the proper methodology for holding a teacup, or other pressing problems of etiquette and propriety.

In 1876, without official sanction, Jardine and Matheson opened China's first railroad. In 1877, the Nanking governor-general purchased the line, ripped up the tracks and ties, and tore down the stations. The locomotives were dismantled, loaded on barges, hauled to Taiwan, and dumped into the surf!

> In your association with the foreigners, your manner and deportment should not be too lofty, and you should have a slightly vague, casual appearance. Let their insults, deceitfulness, and contempt for everything appear to be understood by you and yet seem not understood, for you should look somewhat stupid.[20]

Later Westerners, who viewed the 'heathen Chinee' as simplistic children, would ascribe the destruction of the Shanghai-Wushung Railway to superstition—to a fear that the rails offended the local ghosts. These myopic occidentals simply could not conceive of a Chinese bureaucracy capable of comprehending that a foreign-owned railway system was an intolerable threat to China's otherwise inaccessible heartland.

By the 1870s, Yehonala, a second-rate concubine, had metamorphosed into the Black Widow Empress Tsu Hsi who would seduce, shed, and retake power into the first decade of the twentieth century. It was during her long reign that "the provincial officials obtained much greater freedom of action than ever before."[21] But when her regal majesty raged, no head in the land owned its shoulders.

The trickle of reforms continued. Several diplomatic missions and a few students were sent abroad. A few shipyards tinkered at building a modern navy, and one or two regional bosses encouraged a slow and officially milked industrialization. Then the Western Powers dined again: Chinese Turkestan, Tibet, Korea, and Burma. In 1883-1885 in Annam (Vietnam), China fought the French, but lost. However, this defeat proved a catalyst toward renewed "self-strengthening." Now older, the empress Tsu Hsi sat the callow Emperor Kuang-hsu on the throne, and slipped into the background to pursue her plans for palatial reconstruction.

By 1894, the Western world perhaps saw China as gradually progressing, building her defences, and strong in manpower and theory. Then tiny Japan demolished China's pristine fleet and whipped the Celestial Empire in a lightning war. The Chinese intelligentsia stood aghast, and "there came a great clamor for change" as all-things-Chinese—once sacrosanct—suddenly became terribly suspect.[22]

Earlier cries for radical reforms had been raised, but mostly by unheeded visionaries. Now a substantial number of scholars demanded European math, science, agriculture, a modern army, a national railway system, the telegraph, and a few even dared to whisper of parliamentary monarchy and democracy.

Japan's easy victory had not gone unnoticed by the Western piranha. The French pushed into south-west China from Vietnam. Germany grabbed Kaichow and spread into Shantung. Russia took Port Arthur and part of Manchuria. Britain extended Hong Kong, secured a northern naval base, and consolidated her control over the Yangtse valley. Even Italy launched a fleet.

By 1898, the Celestial Kingdom seemed on the verge of being hacked to pieces, and Emperor Kuang-hsu lent a hopeful ear to the radical intelligentsia. For one hundred days, the young emperor set his vermilion ink to dozens of innovative decrees "without studying the political and social scene."[23] The old empress came out of seclusion, pronounced the boy crazy, swept him into marble imprisonment with the aid of General Yuan Shih-k'ai, and again clamped her talons on the dragon throne!

The idealistic emperor had envisioned elaborate institutional reforms to meet the Western challenge, but the Empress Dowager soon sought a more magical shortcut. However, for all their charms of "invulnerability," the savage "Boxers" fell dead when the lead from Peking's besieged Legation Compound tore into their bodies. The empress ordered her generals to drive the barbarians into the sea and declared war on a major segment of the world!

Several provincial governors wisely kept their troops out of the fray as an eight nation international force broke the siege at Peking, sacked the city, chased the Boxers into the countryside, and again humbled the Celestial Empire. China entered the twentieth century politically and intellectually shattered, drenched in mud, and yoked into the endless "unequal treaties" and the vicious Boxer Protocol with its monumental cash indemnities.

In various multinational consortia, the Western nations quickly rammed a belated Railroad Age into China's interior. By 1910, perhaps six thousand miles of track had been laid.

Of course, the Tsar had a personal train, as did the American president and the British prime minister. So the old empress purchased a sixteen-coach, Imperial Yellow, Royal Train, but for many moons never even set eyes on it. At last, she decreed a journey to Mukden. The throne car, two rolling kitchens, her sleeping chamber, and the coach for a thousand gowns were all lavishly prepared. In case of problems, the empress brought along her leading railroad administrators, so they could instantly be beheaded. They made the trip at an uneventful five miles per. . . .

Her Imperial Majesty Tsze She Duan Yo-kong Yee-Joan Yu-Ghwong Chung-Sho Goong-chin Shen-Tsung She Motherly Auspicious, Orthodox, Heaven Blest, Prosperous,

All-Nourishing, Brightly Manifest, Calm, Sedate, Perfect, Long Lived, Respectful, Reverend Worshipful, Illustrious, Exalted, Empress Dowager,[24] the "Old Buddha" Tzu Hsi reigned concurrently with Britain's Queen Victoria. But in 1908, the "Old Buddha," sometimes called "the only man in the kingdom," finally joined her ancestors, expiring the day before the mysterious death of the too radical young emperor. A toddling nephew, Pu Yi became the Son of Heaven, Emperor of the World, Lord of Ten Thousand Years, and a pawn among princes. A Manchu regent fired the too powerful Yuan Shih K'ai and tried to take charge, but the land was festering with famine and revolt. Plots abounded. Uprisings were suppressed, heads were chopped, but the dynasty was crumbling. On October 10, 1911, one of many bombs of many diverse plotters exploded prematurely and blew the Manchu's Heavenly Mandate to the Netherworld.

To save their hides, the soldiers at Wuchang mutinied and forced their commander, Li Yuan-hung, to lead them. A smouldering anti-Manchu volcano erupted, and Szechwan province led the stampede to secede from the Empire. In a desperate attempt to save the Dynasty, the Manchu regents now summoned Yuan Shih-k'ai.

General Yuan had organized China's modern army and had distinguished himself in Korea but had been "retired" lest his power grow too strong. Coaxed from a feigned lameness back into office, Yuan opened talks with the rebels, but "by December all but a few provinces had declared their independence from Peking and joined in a provisional republican government headquartered in Nanking."[25] In January 1912, Dr. Sun Yat-sen was elected president and Li Yuan-hung was honored with the vice-presidency of this new southern Republic. But civil war seemed likely.

Yuan Shih-k'ai still commanded the loyalty of his former lieutenants, now a military elite in the provinces. Obviously outgunned, Sun Yat-sen made a deal. Yuan would retire the Manchus and govern the nation from southern Nanking. The boy-emperor was forced to abdicate and pensioned off in the palace, and General Yuan became president, but he kept his capital in friendly Peking. A constitution was sketched, a parliament elected and, as director of railway development, Sun Yat-sen began designing an elaborate theoretical railway system.

In 1913, Sun Yat-sen's Nationalist party—the Kuomintang—won a majority in parliament, and a party spokesman named Sung Chiao-jen began criticizing President Yuan's work. Yuan had him rather undemocratically snuffed out. Then, when parliament blocked a scandalous loan, Yuan dismissed the body. Seven provinces again revolted, but this second revolution was quickly crushed. On May 1, 1914, with the adoption of the "Constitutional Compact," Yuan Shih-k'ai—"the father of the warlords"—became a modern military dictator. Then in Serbia, in bagpipe drum and fife, "Great War" bubbled forth.

China quickly declared her neutrality, but Japan joined the Allies and attacked and captured Germany's beachhead in Kaichow. In January 1915, "on paper watermarked with dreadnoughts and machine guns,"[26] Japan presented China with "Twenty One Demands," and President Yuan had no choice but to serve up Manchuria, Shantung and Fukien provinces to the expansive Japanese.

Yuan may have been enjoying a more cosmic vision. While publicly fighting the movement, Yuan was privately fabricating an "Elect Yuan Shih-k'ai Emperor" campaign, complete with ornate petitions and huge gatherings. He finally "reluctantly" agreed to become the emperor of the Celestial Kingdom. Yunnan Province was not impressed, and again revolted. Quickly "overwhelmed by dissent, Yuan reluctantly agreed to retire on June 5, 1916," and died the following day.[27]

If nothing else, Yuan Shih-k'ai had provided a centralizing influence. After his death, no individual had enough charismatic power to hold China's many divergent groups together. The nation shattered into regional factions ruled by military governors, warlords, who grouped and regrouped themselves in a kaleidoscopic barrage of cliques, coalitions, and shifting military alliances. Although Peking continued to house the "internationally recognized" government, several provinces asserted their independence. Various generals luxuriated, and the once Flowery Kingdom sank into a morass of kidnappings, robberies, murders, petty wars, chaos, famine, mud, and anarchy. Of course, Europe wasn't doing too well either.

"A sincere constitutionalist," Li Yuan-hung became the chief of state.[28] But President Li was a figurehead—powerless and irresolute.[29] Two of the contending factions wanted Li out, and a disagreement over China's entrance into the Great War provided the mechanism.

China's premier wanted to arm and join in the European hostilities, so he forced parliament into a belligerent declaration. President Li wouldn't sign it and dismissed the premier. But the provinces again revolted, and to save Peking, President Li invited General Chang Hsun and his troops into the capital.

Still wearing the long Manchu pigtail, General Chang's men entered Peking in July 1917, but instead of "saving the

Republic," old Chang Hsun dusted off the now pubescent former Son-of-Heaven, Pu Yi, and declared the boy Emperor Celestial. This "imperial restoration" lasted until the Anfu and Chihli armies recaptured the capital, about a week later. President Li resigned, Chang Hsun fled, and Pu Yi was again locked away in the palace. The Anfu clique declared war on Germany, and Dr. Sun Yat-sen once again declared an entirely separate southern Republic.

In the spring of 1918, Premier Tuan got his Japanese military aid, but the Great Meaty European War of Attrition was finally grinding to a halt, and China contributed work coolies only. The victors then gathered at Versailles for their vengeance. China sent delegates to France, perhaps seeking the full implementation of Woodrow Wilson's "Fourteen Points" and the return of Shantung province. But a multitude of secret deals had already divvied up the booty, and Japan, for her part in the carnage, was to continue to feast on sacred Shantung.

In early May, when this news reached the chaotic empire, angry demonstrations mushroomed everywhere, and the Chinese delegates to Versailles could not affix their names to the hated parchment.

> For China, the watershed between Yesterday and Today began on May 4th 1919. All my generation date ourselves from that year and day, which means nothing to the Western world, but means everything to a quarter of the world's humanity. For it was the day on which China's intellectuals turned away from the West, because Western democracies killed democracy that year.[30]
>
> Han Suyin

Before the year was out, the first seeds of the Bolshevik Revolution drifted windborne into the withering kingdom.

Following the Armistice, Shantung's Tientsin-Pukow Railway needed new equipment, and U.S. manufacturers again brought in successful bids. In 1919, Alco—The American Locomotive Company—received an order for a dozen 4-6-2 light Pacific passenger engines. These locomotives, #401-412, were built in Schenectady, N.Y., in 1920, and then sent to China. At about this time, the American Car & Foundry received an order for forty-three high class passenger cars—"five complete trains, enameled royal blue and picked out with gold."[31] These new and opulent sleeping and dining cars were, in the summer of 1922, shipped to Shanghai, where their problems began. The Chinese didn't have any ready cash on hand, so these exquisite trains were stored, undelivered, in and around Shanghai's wharves. Finally the foreign railway agents convinced the international banking community to extend a loan to the T-P Railroad. Only then did the elegant Blue Trains begin to roll.

Because of the continued subjugation of Shantung province, the ruling Anfu clique came under attack. In June, Tsao Kun, Wu Pei-fu and a former "Red Beard" bandito, Marshal Chang Tso-lin, met and agreed to bring down the regime. Peking was attacked from two sides, and the Chihli and Manchurian forces easily captured the northern capital.

China, in fact the entire Far East, was a dangerously explosive mess, but this fact had been carefully avoided at Versailles. Now, lest another hideous Great War bubble forth, another major international peace parley was called: the Washington Conference. China received a limited invitation to participate in the "Committee of Pacific and Far East Questions."

The great Washington Conference lasted from November 1921 through February 1922. China's comprehensive suggestions concerning "tariff autonomy; abolition of extraterritoriality; the abolition of spheres of influence; the restoration of leased territories, the withdrawal of foreign armed forces, the railroad guards, foreign police stations, foreign post offices, foreign telegraph and radio stations"[32] were all routinely silenced. To behold Democracy's White Knight eagerly championing China's legitimate rights, see nearly any popular text.

> It was now obvious that no one power alone could keep China down. The agreements concluded at the time of the nine power treaty were designed to ensure a collective system for the maintenance of the status quo, nothing else.[33]

For thirty long years, the Western nations had sung ethereal praises for Japan and her rapid modernization. But the Land of the Rising Sun had learned too quickly, too well. Japan dared to suggest that a clause proclaiming racial equality be added to the charter of the League of Nations. She had practiced racial equality by joining the hitherto "white only" game of grab-all in China, and following World War I, she had emerged as the single most powerful force in the Pacific. To ease this threat, the Western Allies collectively encouraged Japan to return Shantung to the Chinese. Thus confronted, Japan sold her interest in the K-T Railway and began to vacate the province into which Confucius had been born. But although the Chinese delegation had achieved some limited success in Washington, things at home were continuing to disintegrate.

> Sometimes when the subject of China in the good old days crops up, one or other European will say: "Oh, it was the British (or the French, or the Germans, or the Italians) who behaved badly, but we did not. We were always loved by the Chinese. We were not like the others." The truth is, they were all the same.[34]
>
> Han Suyin

Under the rule of the military men the disintegration of China has proceeded with alarming rapidity. And why not? Suppose you are offered a post in the government. Because it is you, let us suppose it to be a high post, such as membership in a cabinet. Suppose you become minister of communications, with the development of all the natural resources— the mines, the forests, the water-power—and the building of all the railroads under your control. Could you want a better opportunity to serve your country?

But you go to the capital. You find no money with which to run your department. Your salary will not pay your living expenses, for there are hordes of people in your family and in your ministry dependent upon you. Nobody in the cabinet dares make a move contrary to the wishes of the particular militarist whose army at the moment controls the city. And that individual is engaged with but one interest. In language that has been heard in other lands, he is "getting his while the getting is good."

One day the general sends for you. There is a foreign concession hunter who wants the control of a certain mine. Will you kindly sign the necessary papers? There will be a large portion of "graft" in it for you if you do. What if the price is ridiculously low? What if it is the general who will profit, and not the people? If you don't sign, you will be punished. Why not take your share of the universal graft?

To the honor of many a Chinese be it said that, confronted by such conditions, scores of them resigned rather than continue in office. . . . Other men were put in their places who were willing to sign anything. . . .[35]

Reverend Paul Hutchinson

Chapter Nine

HAGGLING OVER THE LOOT?

An embattled, embittered President Li began 1923 with a scathing denunciation of the military governors, gangsters, and "generals" who were tearing the empire apart. Li had agreed to assume the Presidency only if the militarists would yield to the Ministry of War. Telegraphic assurances had convinced him that he should once again try to lead the nation. Or at least the northern part of it. Actually, really only the "internationally recognized" northern city-state of Peking, for the Flowery Kingdom now laboriously supported a host of military fiefdoms as well as three major quasi-governments. In Manchuria, Chang Tso-lin ruled a mini-nation, which the

Japanese catered to. At Canton or Shanghai, an off and on parliament under Dr. Sun Yat-sen fought southern warlords and international indifference. At Peking, remained the shattered, pathetic, imperial remnants that the United States and Europe preferred to deal with. Because whoever controlled Peking had access to the several revenues, petty wars and coups abounded. "Then came the Lincheng bandit incident and . . . even political conspiracy was given a few days pause."[1]

> To the Telegraph Office at Lincheng. Just heard Express Train raided by bandits last night. Report immediately all available facts and present situation.[2]

Like the international community, Governor Tien Chung-yu pounced on Lincheng's telegraphic operator as the best source of information. Instantly besieged by irate foreigners, the governor replied with appropriately diplomatic double talk, put a relief train at the foreigners' disposal, and hurried his commander of bandit suppression, Wu Chang Chi, to the scene via the same repair train that carried Naill and Weisenberg. He then busied himself with his maps and his vengeance.

The "Inspector General" of Chihli, Shantung, and Honan provinces, Tsao Kun, ordered the authorities to send in reinforcements and free the foreigners. The governor of Kiangsu sent troops to the border to help, and His Excellency President Li Yuan-hung announced that he would personally pay the ransom.

May 8

"On the morning of the 8th, a regiment of infantry belonging to the 5th Division arrived at Lincheng with machine-guns and field pieces."³ At the mines, Commander Wu Chang Chi, who was arranging his own meeting with the outlaws, put every possible obstacle in the path of Señor Naill and the French and Italian consuls who, nonetheless, made their own trek into the wild.⁴

May 9

A strongly worded presidential mandate appeared, ordering an investigation and indicating that even Shantung's civil and military governors would be punished. Peking's Foreign Ministry told Governor Tien:

> A note has been received from the Diplomatic Corps stating that, according to reports they have received, the troops are pressing against the bandits who raided the train, thus exposing foreign lives to grave danger, and urging the Government to telegraph you to desist from using force but to negotiate for the captives' ransom. Therefore please cease firing for the time being and try to effect immediate release of foreigners by peaceful means. . . .⁵

Meanwhile, more troop-laden trains rolled into Lincheng, onto the spur line, and out toward the coal mines at Tsaochuang.

May 10

Still more reinforcements reached the fortified colliery until, in theory, "the bandits were well surrounded."[6] General Ho, the unofficial commander of the mines, was, himself, well surrounded. In addition to the new troops, Naill and the French and Italian consuls had reached the fortress early on. A Japanese representative and more Americans arrived on the ninth. Family and friends of the hostages came, as did doctors, reporters, industrious hawkers, treasure and thrill seekers, and nebulous agents, and, for the next several days, every train disgorged more.

Desiring to confer on the spot concerning the best means of effecting the release of the captives, a large number of officials assembled at Tsaochuang. Among the military officials may be mentioned General Tien Chung-yu, the Military Governor of Shantung; Cheng Shih-chi, the Commander of the Fifth Division; the Commanders of the 5th, 6th, and 20th Brigades; Sun Tien-yuen, the Defence Commissioner of Hwai Hai, Kiangsu; and Wang Yung-chung, the personal representative of Marshal Tsao Kun. Other prominent officials were Admiral Wu Yu-lin, Minister of Communications; Yang I-teh, Commander of the Police Force in Tientsin; Ting Hung-chao, Superintendent of the Tientsin Police; Wen Shih-chen, Commissioner of Foreign Affairs at Nanking; Feng Kuo-tsao, Managing Director of the Tientsin-Pukow Railway; and the District Magistrates of Teng and Shih. . . .[7]

General Ho Feng-yu did not rejoice in this sudden discovery of his fief. Nor did he welcome an order from

Peking to "consult" with Mr. Naill who was, after all, merely a hireling of a foreign company. He didn't welcome any of the foreign devils, and he didn't trouble himself to hide his displeasure.

May 11

Under intense international pressure, Peking agreed to participate in a "joint inquiry" to ascertain "the circumstances attending the outrage, whether or not there was collusion between the train crew and the brigands, and to fix responsibility of the civil and military authorities."[8]

In Shanghai, Nanking, Tientsin, Mukden, Paotingfu and Erehwon, various Chinese dignitaries and potentates took this day and others to tell the press and the world precisely who was responsible. Tsao Kun blamed the ousted former Premier Liang Shih-i, and demanded that he be "expelled from Hong Kong."[9] Ma Soo, representative of Dr. Sun Yat-sen blamed the old Manchu General Chang Hsun.[10] Some said the right honorable former Red Beard bandito Chang Tso-lin had masterminded the mess. The Anfus, the Japanese, and Governor Tien were all blamed. Many people blamed Tsao Kun.

> "Reports up to the present have indicated that the bandits are standing out for a substantial ransom as well as a guarantee for their own safety. This is apparently incorrect."[11]

The international community and Peking's ersatz officialdom had evidently hoped that freeing the foreigners would be as easy as haggling over a price and forking up the loot. But the messages carried from the mountains by priest, peddler, palanquin, and the "paroled" Jerome Henley set this notion aside. The bandits spoke not of ransom, but of being reinstated in the army.

May 12

Morning. Governor Tien and still more officials, dignitaries, crooks, and cronies rolled into the heavily fortified coal mine, and the cooperative railway freed more luxury sleeping and dining cars onto the protected siding. Jerome Henley's fragile "parole" was about up, and so, in the company of two intrepid negotiators, he left the colliery, soon entering a no-man's land.

Roy Anderson and his incognito associate—educator, linguist, ambassador-in-waiting, and foreign-affairs specialist from Nanking, S. T. Wen—entered the bandit valley with proper pomp, savoir faire, and "face," appropriately chaired by native bearers. Outlaw escorts guided these emissaries into one of the bandit encampments where an elaborate table had been prepared. Only after dining would the chieftain speak: the siege of Paotzuku must be lifted. Some eight thousand confederated brethren must be taken into the national army, although several bandit leaders said nay to this. Some wanted Colonel Kuo T'ai-sheng, uncle of one of the outlaws, to supervise this military re-enlistment. Others wanted their demented former mentor Chang Chin-yao to be made governor of Shantung. Some wanted specie, bucks, coin of the realm, loot, but all demanded that any agreement must be countersigned by the foreign powers. At the witching hour, the diplomatic cosmic clock began to tick in ominous Progressive Indemnity time.

May 13

Wen and Anderson were again laboriously chaired into the bandit valley and ushered along to the Dragon Door Temple. Nestled beside a clear mountain stream, this ancient shrine was the home and temporary prison of "Messrs. Powell, Musso, Friedman and Henley. Major Pinger and Major Allen were visiting the camp at the time."[12]

J. B. Powell, through his years as correspondent for Millard's Review, was acquainted with the Chinese mystery man, Wen Shih-chen, who quickly hushed Powell's enthusiastic welcome. There was time to chat and visit while more than a score of bandit chieftains converged on the sanctuary. Finally a meeting—large and boisterous.

Wen and Anderson suggested that some of the hostages be freed as the siege was lifted, and that the remainder.... But there were too many chiefs, too many voices. Finally, a decision of sorts. The following day, the outlaws would, if possible, hold a meeting, finalize their terms, and elect representatives to a conference with the government officials. But Anderson must guarantee safe passage! And no guns. Progress of sorts, but the sundry miles back to the mines would fill long hours. Later, safe inside the mine's huge walls, Wen and Anderson reported that the outline of a settlement was "acceptable to both sides."[13] Peking's diplomats were informed. Uncle Kuo was summoned. Optimism reigned.

May 14

In an early light, Dr. Paul Mertons left the rescue site for another house call on Guiseppe Musso and friends. Father William Lenfers and a Dutch missionary, Father Bues, made an independent journey into the bush.

An attempt was now made to convene the "joint inquiry" into the derailment, but the Chinese delegate said that he hadn't received any instructions, so work was delayed. This effort may have been overshadowed by the ornate and grandiloquent arrival of Admiral Wu Yu-lin and Commander Yang I-teh.

As Peking's "Minister of Communications," Admiral Wu was, in protocol, the highest ranking Chinese at the site, and he soon accepted progress reports from tuchun Tien and General Ho. Meanwhile, Yang I-teh, boss of Tientsin's police, "denounced all previous efforts made, especially those of tuchun Tien, and told the Chinese and foreign public that he alone was capable of settling the matter."[14]

In Peking, the "government" announced that a "tentative understanding. . . ." But in the mountains, fiery words as thirty-odd outlaw leaders met and argued survival.

When Dr. Mertons entered a rebel camp, several rogues told him to leave, he was not welcome. Mertons demanded and received an audience with several busy chiefs, but they also turned him away. The foreign priests fared no better.

Haggling over the Loot? 113

Later, at the colliery, utterly exhausted, Father Lenfers told the consuls that, contrary to all official Chinese pronouncements, the government troops still had not withdrawn.

The soldiers here, by the way, are having much the worst of the present situation. The bandits have none too much food for a prolonged stay, but the soldiers are actually short already, and have had to put up with small rations for several days.[15]

May 15

Wen and Anderson journeyed into the hills to find out the results of the bandit conference. They found the bandit camp abandoned.

May 16

Counselor Bell wrote to Secretary of State Hughes:

Further consular reports from Lincheng indicate that foreign captives have been taken to Paotzeku and there is nothing to indicate progress in negotiations between Chinese authorities and brigands.[16]

In Peking, the "central government" was angrily reminded of the progressive indemnity. At the mines, tempers were likewise frayed. The foreign consuls resented each other's meddling, and none of them was pleased with the Chinese:

114 Outrage at Lincheng

  Officials of every grade from cabinet minister and tuchun to the most menial underling appeared . . . all, almost without exception, playing politics with only their own private interests in their thoughts, their only concern as to the foreign captives being, how best they might be capitalized to their advantage, with absolutely no concern for the Chinese captives. . . .[17]

  Nor was General Ho thrilled:

  My troops had the bandits surrounded shortly after their raid on the Shanghai-Peking express. If foreign officials had not interfered, I would have told the outlaws if a single foreigner were injured I would cut off the heads of every one of the brigands, down to the last man of the thousands that compose their bands. They know me, and they know I would keep my word. . . . However the foreign officials obliged me to withdraw my troops and the bandits have escaped back into the mountains whither it is almost impossible to follow them.[18]

  Pretty much forgotten in the smoky maze of international complications, the specter of invasion, the ultimatums and dramatic announcements was the health and well-being of the more than one hundred Chinese also taken hostage. A few lucky ones had escaped or had been ransomed by their kin, but the vast majority had been untouched by relief supplies, mail deliveries, or any manifestation of humanitarian concern. Said one tabloid: "It seems that the lives of the Chinese captives are dirt cheap."[19]

  Several bandits came down from their mountains and entered the colliery. Their mission was one of reconnaissance

Haggling over the Loot? 115

but also to invite S. T. Wen and Roy Anderson to a meeting at their stronghold the following day.

Up and down the railway, there were minor battles as allied bandits harassed the government troops or tried to break into the cordon. Reaching the mines on a twenty-four hour parole, Marcel Berube confirmed that, despite all promises, the government troops were actually advancing!

YANG I-TEH AND WU YU-LIN AS HOSTAGES

GOVERNMENT AGREES

(Through Reuter's Agency.)

Peking, May 16

Admiral Wu Yu-lin has sent an urgent wire to the Government today announcing that the foreigners at Lincheng were clamoring for the release of the captives, and the bandits had presented more demands. He says he thinks it necessary that he and General Yang I-teh should go to the brigands' stronghold themselves and offer themselves as hostages in order to obtain the release of the foreigners.

The Government wired granting the request.

Accordingly Admiral Wu and General Yang have gone to the brigand camp.

A mandate has been issued appointing the Vice-Minister of Communications as Acting Minister while Admiral Wu remains a hostage.

May 17

At dawn, a large Chinese entourage trooped out of the mines. General C. C. Ting, Major Lu-lu, and Uncle Kuo were carried in sedan chairs, and "these gentlemen were accompanied by a retinue of about half-a-score of secretaries and coolies who either rode donkeys or walked."[20]

In Peking, several members of parliament grew outspoken in their criticism of Marshal Tsao Kun as the man responsible for the mess. Tsao Kun responded by saying he'd abandon his growing campaign for the presidency to devote his entire energy to solving the crisis. He also discontinued a subsidy he'd been paying the parliamentarians to make up for their pay that had a habit of not coming.

In a "mud hut conference" perhaps a third of the way up the conical Pao Tzu Ku, the outlaws spelled out their demands:

> 1. The withdrawal of all Shantung troops to their original stations. . . . The withdrawal from the province of all extra-provincial troops. . . .
>
> Provided clause 1. is carried out:
>
> 2. Daily supplies are to be dispatched . . . such as food, clothing, arms and ammunition etc. . . .
> 3. That [The People's Liberation Society] be recognized as a separate and independent army and paid as such, and that this district . . . be their location.
> 4. That Sun Mei-yao be appointed Commander-In-Chief of this new army, and Kuo Che-tsai—Chief of Staff.

5. That the agreement be countersigned by the consuls of six foreign powers.[21]

Subject to the approval of his superiors, General Ting agreed to all the proposals except the last. Only four nations were represented at the mines, and they were taking no official part in the negotiations. Instead, Ting suggested that the military governors of several provinces guarantee the agreement.

"You break faith every time!" snapped one of the bandits, and the discussion got ugly. After arguing all night and all through the dawn, the government team left, having concluded nothing.

As soon as General Ting's party was safely out of the way, the surrounding troops again advanced, causing sniping, skirmishes, dead, wounded, and rage when the bandit chiefs again argued strategy. Finally, an ultimatum, and Marcel Berube was launched on a donkey into an impenetrable mountain darkness.

> Despite the high sounding official proclamations, Admiral Wu, the Minister of Communications, and General Yang I-teh of Tientsin, did not leave this morning to give themselves up as hostages for the 16 foreigners still held at the Taoist temple on the slopes of Paotzekou.[22]
>
> The North China *Herald*

May 19

The foreign ambassadors were forwarding notes fast and furious. The foreign press was clamoring for troops, and

China's Foreign Ministry was typically leaderless just when Peking needed an energetic diplomat.

Since April, V. K. Wellington Koo had been the "acting" Minister of Foreign Affairs. As foreign pressure mounted, there was corresponding pressure on Dr. Koo to assume full duties, cool off the foreigners, save China a bit of "face," and minimize the mess. But Dr. Koo had had a year to contemplate Peking's impolite politicking, and he remained aloof. Meanwhile, in southern Shantung, the situation seemed to be moving from bad to worse.

Marcel Berube labored into the mines in the early morning. He told the diplomats of the recent fighting and of the bandits' threat to shoot one British and one American captive if the soldiers weren't withdrawn within four days. Then, as instructed, Berube hurried to Peking to deliver this message to the Diplomatic Body and the President of the Chinese Republic. Admiral Wu Yu-lin and General Yang I-teh likewise sped to the capital for talks with higher authorities.

> As matters stand there is a complete deadlock. The Tuchon has accomplished nothing, the Government's delegation has accomplished nothing, and beyond hindering each other and everyone else, the remainder of the varied Chinese officials have accomplished nothing.[23]
>
> The North China *Herald*

May 20

A military conference was held by Governor Tien and his army officers, at which it was decided to pursue the policy originally agreed upon of inducing the bandits to comply with reasonable terms by waving the big stick over their heads.... Orders were issued for the Fifth Division and other brigades assembled there to press in on all sides....

After having mapped out a plan for military operations and given instructions as to what to do in case of emergency, Governor Tien entrusted the command of the soldiers to his military associate Cheng Shih-chi and left Tsaochuang for Peking.[24]

Chen Wu-wo

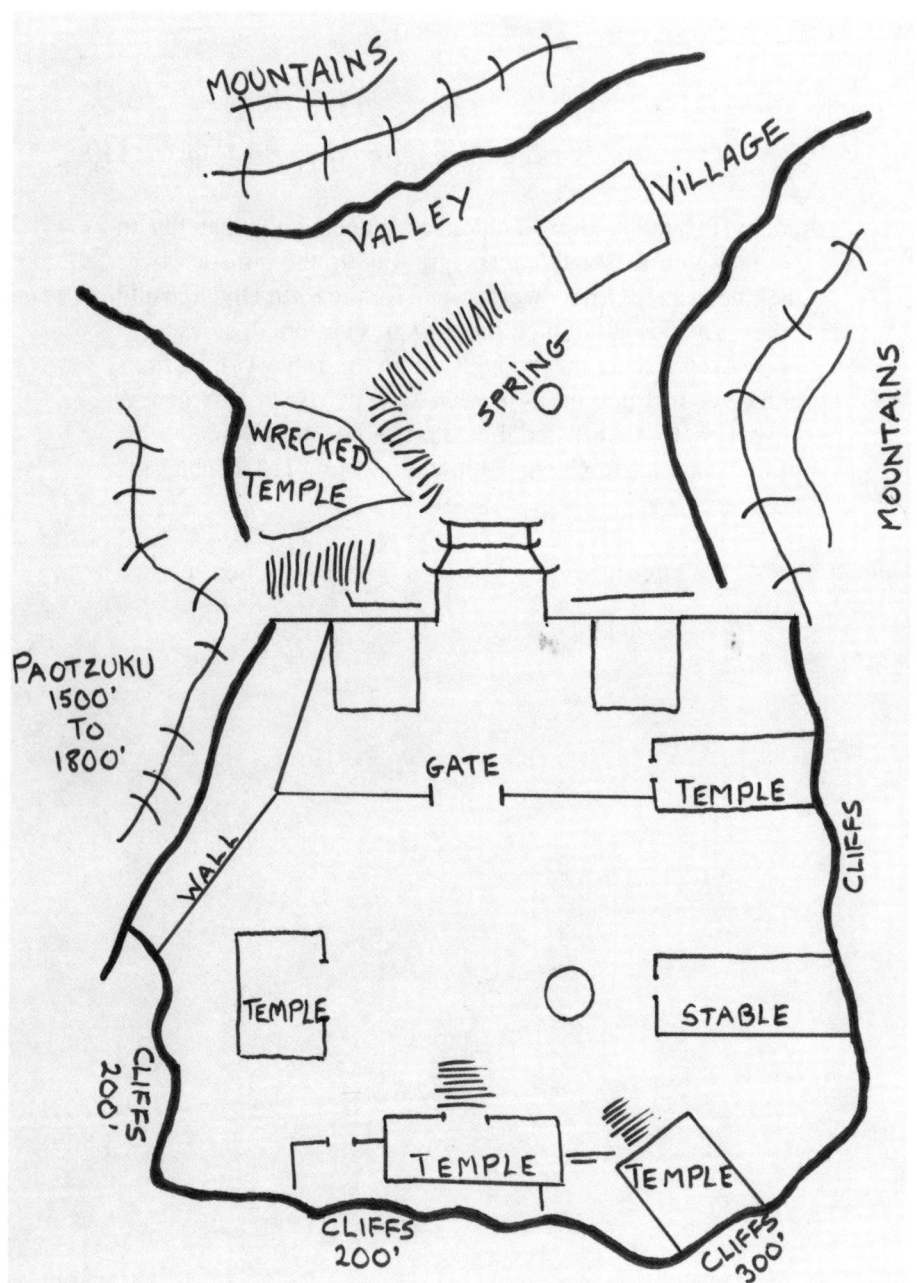

19. The Temples Among the Clouds, drawn by Lee Solomon (Illustration by Ricardo Guerrero Jr.).

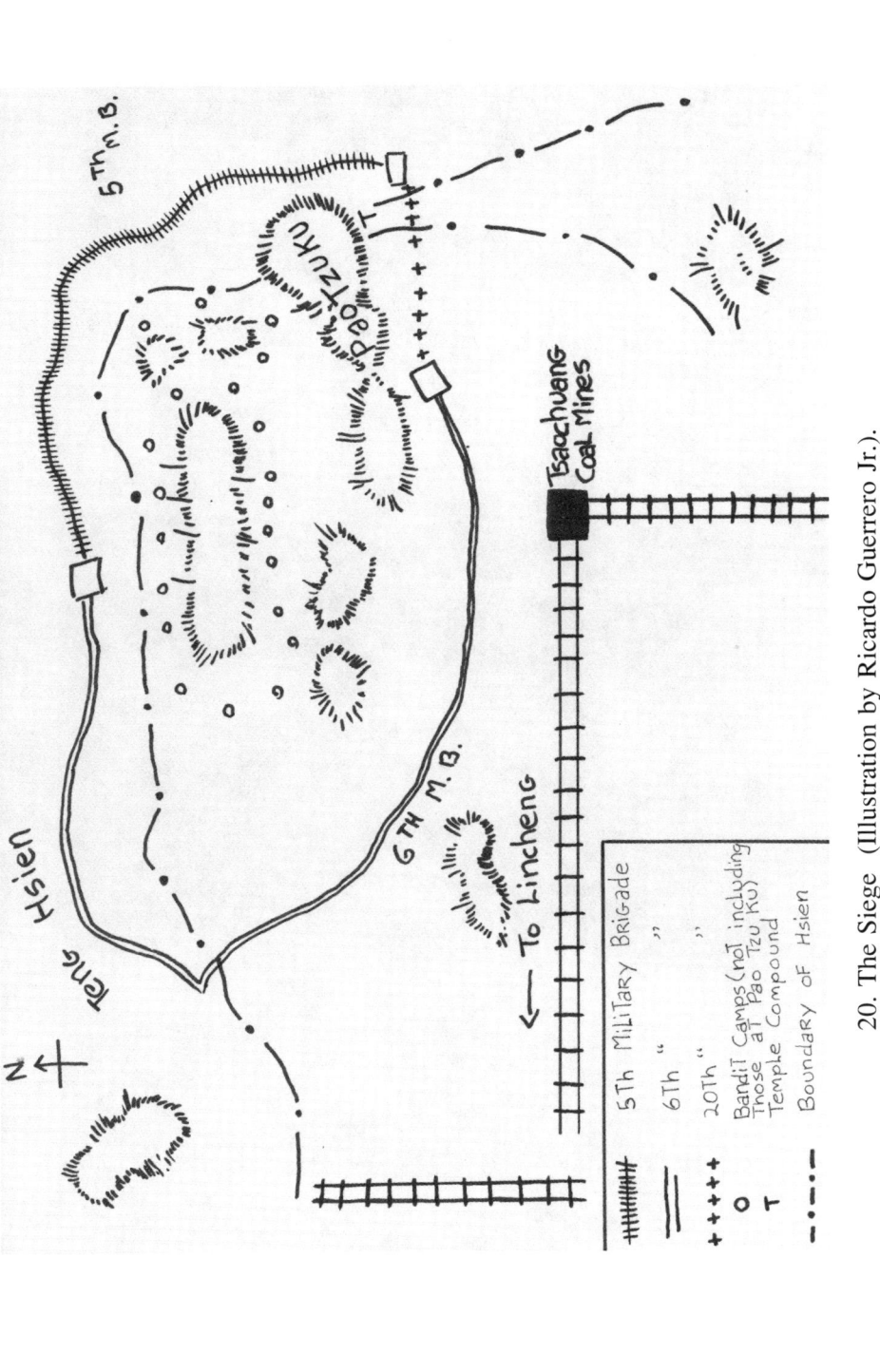

20. The Siege (Illustration by Ricardo Guerrero Jr.).

21. One of the many supply trains leaving the colliery (Courtesy of The Joint Collection, University of Missouri).

22. This is "The Real Red Peril," comments the *Independent News* of Shanghai, referring to the lawlessness occurring throughout China (Illustration by Ricardo Guerrero Jr.).

23. According to *The Citizen*, China is "The Child That Never Grew Up". (Illustration by Ricardo Guerrero Jr.)

24. Fred Elias climbing down from the summit (Courtesy of The Illustrated London News Picture Library).

25. Lee Solomon studying the terrain (Courtesy of The Illustrated London News Picture Library).

Chapter Ten

"THEY USE OUR TOWELS, GLASSES, CUPS . . ."

The mountain top is covered with soft earth, although the mountain is all rock. It is evident that the monks who formerly lived there cultivated quite a farm![1]

Major Roland Pinger

Some of the captives purposely sent out reassuring letters during the first days of their detention, hoping in this way to calm the fears of their friends and relatives. These caused the public to think that our release was only a matter of course. This is a grave mistake. The bandits hold the upper hand and they are absolutely determined to force compliance with their demands for the withdrawal of the troops and the reinstatement of themselves in the army, and they are prepared to forfeit our lives and their own in the attempt[2]

Leon Friedman

It is hell here everyday, every hour, every minute. Some of the bandits who are guarding us are suffering with dysentery, two acutely, while another suffers from an unmentionable disease. They use our towels, glasses, cups and pillows, and drink from our bottles. There are millions of flies. . . .[3]

Guiseppe Musso

Long ago, when devout pilgrims still journeyed here from afar, the monks of this Cloud Nest Monastery tried to sow some vegetables on their mountain's cruel crest. But the soil was mean, hard, in need of fertilizer and a draft animal to break and loosen it, and no ox could possibly be carried up the last hundred jagged meters. But this cloistered clergy had time to gaze out over their valley and the good badlands below. Time to ponder the seasons. Time enough to tarry while a not-too-heavy "calf in hand"—laboriously hauled up the steep cliff—grew into an animal sturdy enough to pull the plow. Paotzuku. Also rendered Pao Tzu Ku. Also Paotzeku, Paotzukuo, Pao-tze-kang. Perhaps a corruption of

Pao Tu Ku, which in Shantung dialect might mean "Calf in Hand." A conical, eerie, volcano-like, holy mountain bandit lair where, by May 20, 1923, in the words of John Benjamin Powell, "all known species of 'cootie' had collected . . . for their annual convention."

Majors Allen and Pinger and mah-jongg manufacturer Lee Solomon passed the night in their buggy stone bunker, but at least they'd had cots, bedrolls, and some food. They'd quickly tidied their new "home," but now the morning revealed a dirty, ugly dugout hovel atop a calf-in-hand mountain in the middle of God-knows-where.

But . . . voices? Visitors! Powell, Friedman, Reginal Rowlatt, puffing a bit from the climb, but laden with greetings from below, canned goods, and some medicine. And any news? And time for tea and talk, and a tour somewhat restricted by otherwise indifferent guards.

Sons of the wealthy in fine silks now tattered and filthy, the Chinese boys mostly just sat and stared into space. Days had turned to weeks and weeks to moons, and with the passing moons, hope had died, leaving the husk—shriveled, ailing children with interstellar eyes. But at least the sun was shining. The view—rugged but nice. Help, freedom, and safety were as near as the colliery, not twenty miles away. Last night they could readily see the mine's powerful searchlight scanning the troubled land.

An hour became two. The rock-climbing guests had chores below, and they didn't want to impose on the limited food supply. So Allen, Pinger, and Solomon—kings of the mountain all—penned quick notes to their loved ones, and the visitors bore these letters down through the great wooden door. Carefully down the skyscraping cliff, down the rugged path. A good hard hike back to the temples. There, in the "mayor's office" in a stall in the barn, they bundled the letters into the outgoing pouch. "For $2.50 gold for the round trip of forty miles, our postman, 'Fazzle Face,' so nicknamed by Crow because of a bad scar, would leave Tsaochuang at 9 o'clock at night and reach our prison camp at about noon the next day."[4]

Fazzle Face or another member of this elite mail service would rest and take nourishment. Then shoulder the outgoing pouch, pass through the pailow archway, and descend the ancient stairway. Through the arbor. Past the tiny ceaseless spring, perhaps a quarter mile to the outlaw village where, the captives believed, their mail was inspected. Through the village, down the tricky frazzled footpath, past bandit lookouts and sentries. To the base. Down. To the valley. There, now all too near, he would enter a no-man's-land between the troops and bandits where stray movement might meet stray bullets. On through the soldiers' scraggly lines. Onward, up, over, down with little shade. The path never easy. $2.50 gold—a good cumshaw for such a lightweight coolie stroll! Hours later, he reached the massive gates of the Sino-German Chung Hsing Colliery. Inside. To the railway cars. To the foreigners.

The following letter was delivered to our representative at Tsaochuang and sent to Mrs. Pinger.

Paozuku Mountain May 20

About 5 p.m. there was a commotion in the camp and the announcement that some or all of us would have to move up to the bandit stronghold on the summit of Pao Tzu Ku. Presently one of the chiefs came along and after much interpretation and talk, it developed that the victims were to be Solomon, Allen and myself. As a matter of fact, I had been selected first, and was entirely packed up before the others knew they were going.

So up we went about 1000 feet, the last 150 or 200 ft. being almost sheer, with hand and toe-holds cut in the sides of the rock. Our captors carried our baggage which has now grown to a respectable size consisting of folding cot, a bedding roll and a couple of small baskets containing food, utensils etc.

We can't imagine the reason for our removal, but understand that negotiations have reached more or less of a deadlock. I think that moving us, all Americans, is something of a gesture on the part of the bandits with a view of securing official American notice. They undoubtedly would welcome foreign intervention as they trust neither the Chinese Government nor the Chinese army.

The first quarters assigned to us were hopelessly foul and already occupied by a bunch of Chinese [probably old prisoners held for ransom.] We expressed our disapproval and then looked around and found a dugout which was fairly clean, although small. We cleaned this out and it is now what I hope will be our last captive home. We are away up in the air, like Talmaipais—high cone-shaped mountain on San Francisco Bay—with the beautiful country spread around us like an artist's map. Nothing but our immediate surroundings suggest the wickedness of man to man. All seems blessed with Sabbath peace below.[5]

May 21

W. K. Naylor, colonel at the predefense War Department, Washington, forwarded a detailed memo on the "possible occupation of the Tientsin-Pukow Railway"[6] to MacMurry, chief of Far Eastern Affairs, State Department. This contingency plan called for placing some twenty thousand additional allied troops in China.

In Peking, Messenger Marcel Berube met with the doyen and those ambassadors who had missing countrymen, confirmed that the Chinese troops had never been withdrawn, and spoke of the execution of one American and one Britisher if the siege wasn't lifted by Tuesday—the morrow. The diplomats were soon penning a stern note.

Roy Anderson and Governor Tien reached the capital in the evening. Anderson met for three hours with Dr. Schurman, and tuchun Tien sought President Li's guidance concerning his delicate dilemma:

> [1] Fight the bandits and foreigners may be killed; [2] withdraw troops to points designated by bandits and confederate bandits will pour in from the three neighboring Provinces of Honan, Kiangsu and Anhui, and together take possession of south western Shantung. . . . [7]

Even with the troops, miners, railway men, consular staff, politicians, militarists, newsmen, family, and friends gathered at the mines, the day remained subdued; the real bosses had all gone to Peking. In the hills: no talks, some shooting, and yesterday's coolie caravan of goodies had only been allowed as far as the foothills. There was no telling what, if anything, had reached the prisoners. Optimism had vanished. There was bickering among the consuls, and there simply wasn't a lot to do except outfit another coolie train and dispatch and distribute the mail. An incoming note from globe-trotting old William Smith. . . .

> The high chief and two minor chiefs were here again this morning, and he shook hands with me and renewed his promise that I should be released the first time anyone was sent down to the station. Of course, this conversation was through an interpreter, a captive Chinese, Mr. Chi Chang, who was educated in England, and is a Cambridge University man of very pro-English sentiments. . . . I should dearly like him to accompany me out, and as he is not a foreigner, I see no reason why he should not. If a ransom, say of $700 was demanded I would pay it out of my account. Could you communicate with the head chief, the elderly man who seems to have some of the milk of human kindness in him?[8]

Drinking heavily, nervous, sullen, some of the renegades were indeed running low on the elixir of decency. There'd been shooting as the soldiers and outlawed former soldiers probed each other's lines, and the lines were in the valley of the shadow. Far above, on the mountain's fortified summit, the coal mine's powerful searchlight may have already clearly been seen to blink.

May 22

The morning clouds and mist were hovering near the withering temples. Looking "more like bandits than the bandits themselves" in their donated, bartered, and borrowed bits of clothing and with wild beards sprouting, the captives soberly discussed the current deadlock and decided to meet with the bandit leadership to see if there were any way of helping matters.

Dr. Siji C. Hung's heels had blistered and abscessed, and the foreign captives had operated with "an old safety razor blade fastened to a piece of wood."[9] He thus hobbled down the mountainside to the outlaw village for a preliminary parley. At about this time, said Powell:

> I was digging into a parcel of raisins marked with my name when I found a note written on thin paper, carefully folded and secreted in the center of the box. The note came from an American army officer. . . .
> In view of the mounting indignation at the delay in releasing the captives, the officer asked me to sound out the other captives regarding a daring rescue scheme which had been proposed. According to the plan which he unfolded, the rescue party at the coal mine would secretly bring to the nearest railway a contingent of about fifty United States soldiers and marines. They would be brought from Peking and Tientsin in small groups, attired in plain clothes so as not to attract attention. But first the carrier-coolie who brought in our food would smuggle in to us, concealed in boxes of raisins, a number of revolvers and a supply of ammunition. When all was in readiness . . . we would proceed to one of the caves in the cliff back of our temple, barricade the entrance, and prepare to stand off the bandits until our rescuers could make the forty-mile raid through the mountains. . . .[10]

In the valley, the first cherries were ripe, the kaoliang sorghum was growing rapidly, and the firearms were silent.

With two field and five machine guns, troops from the Chihli army had arrived and relieved the fifth and sixth Shantung brigades. Casualties had been light—one Shantung soldier bayoneted one of the unwelcome reinforcements. Meanwhile, in the northern capital, Governor Tien called for firmness:

> If the Government should decide upon suppression, then I will not shrink from the task, no matter how difficult it is.
>
> If the Government should decide to yield to the bandits, then I must enter a vigorous protest and request the Government to appoint a more capable man to handle the situation, while I shall wait in Peking to receive my due punishment.
>
> I shall be waiting for the instructions of the Government as to what to do.[11]

China's minister of communications met with the American, British, French, Italian, and Mexican ambassadors and likewise stated that "a show of force was essential to the success of any negotiations."[12]

Dr. Schurman, who'd earlier praised the efforts of the Chinese officials, found Admiral Wu's performance very unsatisfactory.[13] Said the shrewd newsman Rodney Gilbert:

> Having weathered the first storm of wrath safely without calling down upon themselves anything more serious than threats of indemnities and "urgent" notes [the Chinese officials] have settled into their own stride and have already opened the usual campaign of passive resistance, following the usual policy of polite assurances, evasion, procrastination, shifting of responsibility, division of the enemy's camp,

to be followed at last by the politely but stubbornly expressed stand of "what are you going to do about it?"[14]

Various politically active Chinese suggested that the international community withdraw its recognition from the moribund Peking "government."

May 23

Several local Chinese gentry now journeyed into the bandit lair to urge a moderate, middle way. The outlaws expressed surprise at the lull in negotiations and promised to soon send delegates to the mines. Through the good Father Bues, the chiefs also requested that the relief center once again ship up the tabloids.

It had been no great secret that an educated handful of outlaws were reading the British and American newspapers being sent in for the captives' convenience, but it was now "decided by the relief party to delete all news of the Lincheng outrage."[15] Scissors were thus selectively applied.

In Peking, the exasperated foreign diplomats decided to dispatch a commission of top-ranking military men to the scene. They also decided "to instruct the consuls at Tsaochuang to get into touch with the bandit chiefs and acquaint them with the following resolution of the Diplomatic Body:

> That if the release of the captives is delayed or withheld owing to the refusal of the brigands to accept reasonable terms offered them by the Chinese authorities, the foreign

Governments will hold the brigands responsible with their lives for any fatal consequences which may ensue to their nationals as a result of such delay or refusal to treat.

The consuls were further instructed that in communicating the above they were to make it quite clear to the brigands that they were not authorized to enter into negotiations with them or give any form of guarantees.[16]

May 24

Several chieftains hiked up to the temples for informal talks. The captives seem to have gone on the offensive, demanding that their compatriots be brought down from the mountain top, pressing the bandits to honor their repeatedly broken promise of granting freedom to old man Smith, and warning of an overwhelming foreign military force. But in Peking:

> In view of the continued deadlock in negotiations, the Diplomatic Body met again. . . . The dispatch of foreign troops to the scene had been vociferously demanded by a section of the foreign public in China, and the practicability of this proposal was considered and rejected. . . . Unless our Governments were prepared to use a very considerable measure of force and run the risk of very serious complications, it was obvious that such a proposal could only be carried into effect with the consent of the Chinese Government, by whom it would inevitably be resisted. . . . Letters received from the captives made it quite plain that any such move would immediately endanger their lives.[17]
>
> Sir Ronald Macleay

The American State Department had reached a similar conclusion, and Secretary Hughes forwarded Dr. Schurman's latest reports to President Harding, who was perhaps more interested in a gurgling Teapot Dome.

After discussions with President Li and Premier Chang, and after making a special trip to see Tsao Kun, Governor Tien finally received his government's definitive instructions "Hsiang-chi Pan-li—Act according to circumstances."

Six miles north of the mines, there was fierce firing as yet another band of renegades tried, without success, to break into the government cordon.

May 25

On top of the "calf in hand," wee knife in hand to help whittle away the long hours, Lee Solomon carved a plaque christening their hobo home the "S A P C L U B." In a note to the consul staff, Major Pinger reported that, following an attack of indigestion, he was feeling better, but complained about the lack of exercise and asked if the center could send up some "medicine balls, baseballs," hand grenades? "The 'Captives' Club' won the mah-jongg championship of Paotzeku from the Association of Bandit Chieftains states Major Pinger."[18]

The outlaw chiefs now prepared yet another statement of their terms. J. B. Powell was informed that he'd soon be paroled to the mines, and a horse was ordered readied for the journey.

Below the bandit village, shots rang out as drunken sentries stupidly fired at two delegates from the local gentry.[19] These learned gents jumped from their palanquins and flashed desperate peace signs. They were searched and marched to headquarters.

At the Cloud Nest Shrines—boredom, tedium, trepidation, mundane chores, chatter, books from a "circulating library," in-coming and out-going mail. Long before May 25, probably to comfort his companions, publisher Manuel Verea had related several stories from his two previous kidnapping experiences. Both occured in his native Mexico, both times at the hands of nonpolitical banditos who promptly released him for a generous ransom. With the aid of the still ailing Guiseppe D. Musso, attorney at intrigue, Leon Friedman executed his Last Will and Testament and dispatched it to the mines.

Poised to "act according to circumstances,"

> General Tien Chung-yu returned to Shantung on May 25 to make detailed plans and to direct in person the execution of his program. In the meantime the Government was asked to instruct the Aeronautical Department to immediately dispatch to Tsaochuang three aeroplanes for scout duty as a preliminary to the vigorous prosecution of the policy decided upon. More troops were rushed to Tsaochuang and the Military Governor of Kiangsu was asked to render support and active assistance.[20]

The "horse" supplied to J. B. Powell was actually a Shantung mule with a razor-edged backbone. After twenty terrible miles, Powell trailed into the mines at about 6:15 P.M.

I called upon the American consul, Mr. Davis, and by him I was introduced to the Pang-pan. . . . I handed him the terms that the chieftains had given me.

Early the next morning, I set out on my return journey to the bandit camp. The Pang-pan . . . told me that he would personally guarantee absolute safety to any negotiators the bandit chieftains desired to send. . . .[21]

May 26

Peking's Diplomatic Corps appointed its representatives to the "International Military Commission," and told the Chinese government to do the same.

In "Some Additional Reflections," the Peking and Tientsin Times printed some timely thoughts concerning terrorism.

> The Chinese have a proverb that "a three year's famine will not starve the cook," and if worse comes to worst, it is plain to be seen whose hunger, on that mountain top, will first receive attention. On the other hand, if ample supplies are sent up, the robbers, having nothing to complain of, can probably stand the present situation as long as anybody. They clearly hold the winning hand. Some, both Chinese and foreigners, advocate a direct attack on the bandit stronghold, even if such a step does mean death to some of the captives! Their arguments would probably be considerably modified if they themselves spoke from, not of, Paotzuku.[22]

Via the fledgling National Aeronautical Department, two Aero scout planes now descended on Lincheng, and additional troops from Anhui, Honan, and Chihli provinces converged on Shantung's border panhandle.

An adventuresome journalist, Edna Lee Booker was apparently the only foreign woman to visit the mines. Since her beat tended toward the Society pages, she soon headed to Peking where she caught up with the recuperating Lucy T. Aldrich.

> Miss Aldrich was concerned over her rings. One was a large diamond solitaire, the other a valuable emerald.
> In the Peking hospital, Miss Aldrich drew a map of the bandit trail, marking as best she could the spot where she had hidden them, and it was sent to the Standard Oil office in Tsinan, a short distance from Lincheng. Although the mountains were honeycombed with trails, covered with boulders and rocks, searchers were sent out on what came to be known as the jewel hunt. . . .

According to the North China *Herald* of June 9:

> After Miss Aldrich's rescue by Mr. Naill of the Asia Development Co.'s staff, she gave him a rough map of where she had hidden her jewels and Mr. Naill handed the map over to Mr. Babcock, the Standard Oil Co.'s representative in Tsinanfu, who started out soon after in search of them.
> Although Mr. Babcock roamed the Shantung hills for nearly three days he was unable to locate Miss Aldrich's property, principally because her sketch map was only roughly drawn and left out necessarily many of the most important landmarks. He returned to Tsinanfu and told his No. 1 boy of his difficulty, and offered him a substantial reward if he could find the jewels. . . .

"They Use Our Towels..."   135

According to Edna:

Feeling that his master, who was the number one of the Standard Oil office at Tsinan, would lose much face if the rings were not recovered, the houseboy set out to find them. The one clue he possessed was that the rings were hidden on the mountain "where the old one was shot in the neck." He could make few inquiries, however, for the country people, many of whom were bandits or related to bandits, were as suspicious as Kentucky mountaineers. . . .

After hiring a bandit cousin as a guide and changing into a faded cotton coat such as a poor farmer might wear, he set off. For several days he combed the trail slowly and carefully. He forgot his dignity and lifted rocks, grubbed in the earth. . . .

Or, via the Herald:

Last Saturday [Mr. Babcock and his number one boy] returned to Lincheng, and early on Sunday morning set out again on the search. They tried their best to trace Miss Aldrich's route from the time she left the train until she was rescued. Late that afternoon, when they had almost given up the search after wandering over the countryside for many miles, the boy stumbled against a short flat rock, dislodging it. . . .

Or, as Edna relates:

He sank down on the trail exhausted and discouraged: he must return to his master's house a failure. As he sat bowed in misery, his hand touched. . . .[23]

Said the Herald:

> Miss Aldrich's handkerchief, soiled and crumpled but containing her diamond and emerald rings valued approximately at Gold $50,000.

And/or

After a dreadful surrealistic wheelbarrow ride, at a railway station in the newly industrialized town of Tseet-sun, warm, clean and comfortable, thanks to the kindness of the Station Master's wife and daughter, Lucy Aldrich sketched a map to her buried treasure and entrusted this drawing to Señor Naill. Naill wisely passed the map to Babcock of Standard Oil. Babcock personally searched and then initiated a still larger search—jocularly known as "The Jewel Hunt"—which went on, and off, and on again for a fortnight. It was one of Mr. Babcock's trusted employees, a Chinese, a Han, who after painstaking hard work, with joss actually found the Aldrich heirlooms on Sunday, May 27, 1923.

Although the bandit leadership included classically and internationally educated gownsmen and sophisticated military planners, the rank and file were perhaps a bit rank: "the lowest type of coolies,"[24] prone to garlic, spittle, amulets, and superstition. More than one of the privates had greased a priest's palm for "divine protection" in the form of a "chest screen," proclaiming: "Buddha hereby orders his Generals Hung and Ha to protect the person who carries this charm."[25] The same type of "bullet-proof-bib" the half-crazed Boxers had worn!

A mite more for political rather than devotional reasons, the renegade headmen likewise honored the gods, and "the bandit chief has promised to rebuild the temple and to give a great celebration that will last for two whole months with actors and great feasting if the present enterprise wins out. . . ."[26] But for now, the nitty gritty circumlocution of negotiation.

Tall and dignified in his blue silk, sporting a rare red mustache, Liu Yu-kang was said to be a direct descendant of Confucius. Chi Chen-chiang, also attired in a gown, was rumored to have been a commander in the army of Feng Yu-hsiang, the "Christian general," who probably didn't baptize his men with firehoses. Both men were fluent in English and "secretaries" of the Alias Society. Both men were in the delicate protection of J. B. Powell's word of honor and that of the Pang-pan.

It was after dark when Powell and his wards reached the mines. General Cheng Shih-chi, the Deputy Governor, and his military advisor greeted the bandit emissaries with courtesy and escorted them into one of the railway cars for private talks. An hour later, without dramatic announcement, the outlaw-scholars retired to "Mr. Anderson's car where a dinner was given for them."[27]

Having walked many mountain miles in the three previous days, Powell was in no hurry to plunge back into the bush, so it was arranged that the "secretaries" spend the night as guests of the American consul.

> After the bandits had retired to their compartment, we heard a commotion. Then the old Cantonese cook, who had

been serving meals for the American relief party, came rushing in to Mr. Davis in great indignation and cried that the bandits had demanded a bath before going to bed. He said that it was beneath his dignity to prepare a bath for bandits. . . .[28]

May 28

The bandit representatives wanted to do some shopping, so several foreigners escorted them into the nearby town. After appropriate bargaining, the secretaries picked out some mandarin blue silk, ankle bands, hose supporters, and satin slippers and paid coin-of-the-realm, admitting that it was a "novel experience" to do so but that they did pay for their acquisitions "whenever possible."[29] Then back to the colliery, and the deputy tuchun magnanimously ordered sedan-chairs readied. Powell and his guests left the mining compound shortly after noon. The bandits carried a copy of the Pang-pan's suggested terms of settlement.

At about 3:00 P.M., much to everyone's surprise, Powell and his entourage returned to the mine. After being joggled over the hills for a long hour, they had reached the last government lines where the troops demanded their passes. Lacking written authorization, they were turned back.

> The old Pang-pan was profuse in his apologies—orders had been given to tighten up the military lines that morning and he had forgotten to give us passes—and so on. He was "very sorry" and "very sorry," until I felt that a mistake had really been made.
> Finally the passes were ready and we started out again. As I went by the American supply car, I saw Roy Anderson laughing to himself. "Powell, that was a dirty trick to play on

you," he said, "but that old Pang-pan has certainly impressed those bandits with the strength of his military lines."[30]

In the ancient bandit fortress of Pao Tu Shan, there was crazy fearful running about and rapid technological enlightenment when dragonfly demons came diving out of the sky, buzzing the bandit camps and belching leaflets ordering the outcasts "to accept peaceful mutual bargains otherwise bombs will be thrown down to exterminate them next time."[31]

May 29

Governor Tien returned to the mines either the morning of the 29th or the evening of the 28th. He was not pleased to see the innumerable sharp-eyed hawkers of Chinese sundries and ordered them out.

Into the prison plateau, now clockwork every second day, came a coolie caravan of cracker-jack goodies for the foreigners. Into the hills, able to kill one and all, came several artillery pieces.

Meanwhile, in Peking, sundry members of the International Military Commission were "cooling their heels."[32] Peking's designated representative to the commission had declined the job. Then, too, the Chinese railway was having some difficulties assembling a special train worthy of such a multinational entourage.

Midnight. The mine's powerful searchlight was scanning the land, although, due to the hour, probably not blinking its Morse code to the majors up top. A lone mounted figure. An exhausted J. B. Powell with a note for the authorities.

May 30

In the morning, Anderson, Powell, S. T. Wen, and others entered the agreed upon village and "were greeted by a large body of bandits and a somewhat spasmodic fanfare on the solitary bugle."[33] A quick chat, then still deeper into the bandit lines to another village and a second quasi-military marshaling. Some flum and flattery, then down to negotiations.

The government representatives wanted a gesture of good faith from the outlaws and asked for the unconditional release of William Smith, whose freedom had been promised earlier. The outlaws, in their wisdom, agreed to free Smith and Major Allen as well—the "gray-haired ones." Furthermore, the chieftain decreed that Solomon and Pinger, who along with Allen shared the Paotzuku Penthouse, could now rejoin their comrades at the more comfortable Cloud Nest Shrines. The chiefs jotted a note to this effect and dispatched it to the nearby mesa. More than likely, tea was served.

The chiefs had patriotic friends in neighboring hills who also desired reenlistment, but the circle of soldiers made reunion difficult. But no, the government troops would remain. However, when the men of Paotzuku—the men with rifles—signed the muster list, regular shipments of victuals would begin. The chiefs were not pleased with the continuing siege but. . . . Some of the brethren were outfitted with pistols, and surely they shouldn't be excluded from honorable service. This issue—"Is a Revolver A Rifle"—was kicked back and forth, but finally deferred until a later date. "The bandits then demanded that any agreement should be witnessed and guaranteed by the group of foreign consuls assembled at Tsaochuang. It was then explained to them, at great length, how impossible it would be for the foreign consuls to act as guarantors. . . ."[34] Roy Anderson, however, suggested that he might be able to underwrite the agreement. The outlaws, who were coming to trust Mr. Anderson, were moved.

When Major Allen was informed that he was free and that Major Pinger and Lee Solomon should likewise begin packing, they didn't believe it. They thought it some kind of ruse, so, in true Chinese fashion, said they'd grown attached to their little home. They had put in a lot of work fixing up the paths and making everything pretty, and they'd rather stay put but thanks anyway. But the outlaws were reassuring and insistent, so Major Allen packed his gear, including an old sword he'd traded for a box of cigars, and Solomon grabbed the "Sap Club" sign. Down they came.

The Cloud Nest gang gaily welcomed Solomon and Pinger back into the fold and had hearty goodbyes for Smith and Allen, who were escorted through the pailow and down the steps. Hours later, at liberty and safe at the mines, Major Allen said that he was very much looking forward to joining his family. He was otherwise militarily mum[35] and quietly slipped away.

"We never showed the white feather, even in the darkest hour," glowed William Smith, sun tanned, jubilant, and charming in his army garb. "The Manchester sexagenarian" was more than delighted to dip into his basket of souvenirs and to indulge in eloquent elocution with staff and reporters. "When I was leaving Paotzeku," said a thoughtful Smith, "I had a mixed feeling of joy and regret. Joy over my release, but regret for losing the companionship of some of the finest and truest spirits that it has ever been my good fortune to meet. . . ."[36]

May 31

The colliery was now much more of an army base than a coal mining establishment. To this camp returned the tough old German missionary, Father William Lenfers. His Holiness Pope Pius XI had telegraphed to say that Lenfers should return to the hills and secure freedom for Commodore Musso. But consul staff asked him to wait a bit. The talks were going well, and the good priest's sudden appearance just might spook the touchy outcasts.

A mile into renegade turf was Wu Chia Ho, a tiny wrecked hamlet, where further negotiations were to take place. There, Wen and Anderson introduced the military men and sundry gentry to the several chieftains, offered encouragement, and then withdrew.

The outlaws wanted thousands and other thousands of their brethren reinstated in the army. The deputy Pang-pan suggested that the number be limited to those gentlemen actually having rifles and currently residing within the cordon. But Bo-bo Liu and his bunch didn't want enlistment at all. The government offered them pardons so they could return to their homes, but these hardened rogues thought they should receive a settlement to help restore their shattered lives—a million dollars seemed sufficient.[37]

"They Use Our Towels . . ." 143

Meanwhile, on the nearby mesa, the "Sap Club" was by no means a thing of the past. It is now under canvas in the inner courtyard of the temple. With a fly erected in the front of the veranda, it is already the social centre of the camp. The little sign hangs in front on the tent pole, and above the A is punched a little star in memory of Allen, the first charter member to go on the nonresident list. Solomon has agreed that the last man here gets the sign.[38]

ANOTHER AEROPLANE

Peking, June 1.

A large aeroplane left Peking yesterday for Lincheng. The military mission left for Lincheng this afternoon - Reuter.[39]

Possibly as the result of the communication made by the consuls to the brigands, supported by the arrival of the foreign military mission, a welcome change began to be apparent at the beginning of this month in the attitude of the brigands, who seemed at last to be realizing that there was a limit to what they could get in return for their foreign hostages.[40]

Sir Ronald Macleay

26. While the foreign powers goad the Chinese government, the monkey bandit dangles out of reach (Illustration by Ricardo Guerrero Jr.).

27. J. B. Powell, Commodore Musso, and Lee Solomon released by the Chinese bandits (UPI/Bettmann Newsphotos).

28. After being ransomed: (left to right) Professor Cheng, Mr. H. Gensburger, Mr. E. Gensburger, Mr. J. B. Powell, Mr. Lee Solomon, Mrs. Hung, Mr. L. Friedman, Mr. Charles Cheng, and Mr. Fred Elias (Courtesy of The Illustrated London News Picture Library).

29. (left to right) Commodore Musso, J. B. Powell, and Lee Solomon arrive at the Nanking ferry following their release (Courtesy of The Illustrated London News Picture Library).

30. End of train showing metalwork (Courtesy of American Car & Foundry).

31. Carl Crow designed similar five and fifty cent stamps, which were used on letters and parcels destined for the bandit camp. The rebels respected these stamps, which later were much in demand by collectors all over the world.

32. Journalist J. B. Powell back on the job (Courtesy of The Joint Collection, University of Missouri)

33. An educated Chinese bandit in a new military uniform: "Ah! Ah! Ah! Shakespeare was right—what fools these mortals be!" Shanghai *Times*. (Illustration by Ricardo Guerrero Jr.).

Chapter Eleven

INTERNATIONAL PRESSURE

A once opulent clan enclave, Wu Chih Ho was now gutted, all in ruins but two rooms. To this hamlet came General Chen Tiao-yuan and Colonel Huang representing the Pang-pan and the powers that be, or powers that would or could be. Speaking for the honorable Aliases were Sun Mei-yao, Kuo Chih-tsai, and Bo-bo Liu, with others afoot. The government men brought along several local gentry, plus four skilled scribes to paint down the names of those Aliases returning to active duty. Bo-bo packed a tiny pistol.

Delayed since the middle of May, the "Joint Inquiry" into the derailment held its opening meeting at the mines. It was soon obvious that the instructions the Chinese delegation had received were much narrower than the mandate issued to the British, American, French, and Italian consuls.

In Washington, Secretary of State Charles Evans Hughes discussed Schurman's report of May 26 with Warren G. Harding. President Harding agreed "that any attempt to bring comprehensive armed pressure to bear upon China would be useless,"[1] and Hughes sent Schurman a detailed statement of policy. While cool to the idea "of foreign occupation of the railroad from Tientsin to Pukow,"[2] Secretary Hughes indicated that limited force might be applied if the objective were clearly defined and if such action would increase foreign prestige.[3]

At Wu Chih Ho, midway between the colliery and the prison monastery, Bo-bo Liu took exception to his confederates spirit of compromise. He mocked his brethren's desire for reenlistment in the army. He snapped at General Chen's intervention and pulled his pistol and would have blasted Chen if Sun Mei-yao and Kuo hadn't restrained him. Even so, "the conference was all but broken up."[4]

A puff and a breather, then various subconferences that yielded an unwritten, initial deal. The chiefs of the honorable Aliases would accept the rifles and qualifying pistols of any brethren who wished to be "disbanded" and, in the coming days, the eyes of the surrounding troops wouldn't look hard at any "unarmed coolies" leaving the hills. Nor would grubby fingers frisk for booty. This delicate issue now nearly resolved to Bo-bo's satisfaction, the delegates pressed on.

At the urging of his bishop, Father Auguste Potte, a German medical missionary, made his way to the Pao Tzu Ku to try again to secure freedom for Signor Musso. But the bandits thought he came as a spy and told him to go away. Father Potte was practiced in Chinese etiquette, however, so he talked and smiled and explained about his duty, and while the outlaws wouldn't free the Commodore, they finally did allow this stubborn priest to take up residence in the Temples Among the Clouds.

> Pursuant to "Memorandum of Instruction for Guidance of the International Military Commission," from the Dean of the Diplomatic Body, entire membership left Tientsin, Chihli at 8:27 p.m. June 1st in special cars furnished by Ministry of Communications and attached to the "Shantung Express" of that date. The special cars were detached at Lincheng and proceeded to Tsao Chuang. . . .[5]

Several rumors past dark, a guarded foreign journalist nosed his way into Wu Chia Ho. The little wrecked hamlet was still bustling as messengers came and went, soldiers mingled with former soldiers, scribes puttered with papers, and the chiefs and government men wrangled on. One Chinese officer said that excellent progress had been made and that certain foreigners would be freed. After several uneventful hours, the foreigner and his bodyguards returned to the pits.

With dawn, a hopeful but fruitless all night vigil came to an end at the colliery. Rumors of freed foreigners had arrived, and sedan chairs had been sent out, but as yet, no captives. Now a mail-coolie laden with letters and pidgin poop of foreigners who'd left the mountain.

At about 11 A.M., the watchtowers announced a large party. In the homestretch: two liberated "car boys," a Chinese medical student, and the manager of the mine's nephew, who'd been kidnapped from town. These gentlemen were soon followed by General Chen and his entourage, some gentry, several outlaws, and, finally, Señor Verea, Theo Saphiere, Eddie Elias, and Jerome Henley.

Kettles and cauldrons to the stoves! Yes, their comrades on the Cloud Nest were well. A twenty minute warning was all they'd had. Freed at dawn. A bit of quick packing, a hasty good-bye, and down they came. Manuel Verea showed off his cuff links, the very ones he'd brought to China from Mexico. But that was all that remained from all the trunks and suitcases, and he'd only salvaged these baubles because Reginal Rowlatt had "bought them from one of the bandits for $2."[6] But nearly to the day, it was his first wedding anniversary, and what a beautifully free mañana he would share with his Señora!

Above, and still a rarity in 1923, an aeroplane or airplane. A biplane? Lunch, for some a feast, and into this festive atmosphere came the huff puff puff of the special train bearing the International Military Commission: General William Conner, commanding the American troops in China; Lieutenant Colonel H. B. Orpen-Palmer, British military attaché; Colonel E. Sautel, commanding the French troops of North China; Colonel Uyeno, representing the Japanese Command; and Capitaine De Corvette Jachino, Italian naval attaché. Plus staff.

Upon arrival, Brigadier Generals Ho Feng-yu, Li Shen, Wu Chang Chi commanding respectively the 6th, 5th and 20th Brigades . . . were present at the siding with an escort of honor. The Commission forwarded its cards to the Deputy Military Governor and at 3:30 p.m. his official call was made, which was promptly returned.[7]

Meanwhile, Kuo and Sun met with Anderson and Wen and the cronies of tuchun Tien. The various reporters called upon the freed foreigners, who'd already chatted with their consuls, who'd briefed the newly arrived military specialists, who were making contact with the sundry Chinese officials, who conferred in their several subfactions while the sun and clock went round and round.

An agreement seemed near. Approximately three thousand armed Honorables would receive uniforms, commit their names to the muster list, and join the fifth Division. Pay and back-pay of fifty thousand silver dollars would magically levitate itself into the hills, and the foreigners would be released "when the agreement was formally signed."[8]

Sadly, while enjoying his liberated rounds in the various dining cars, Theo Saphiere slipped and fell onto the rails. "He was badly bruised, and was attended by the Red Cross section."[9]

June 3

When the Military Commission first interviewed the Chinese commanders, the foreigners found that "none of these officers seemed to know very much about the location of their troops, the number of same, or how they were disposed." Thus "it was decided to make a mounted reconnaissance on the morning of June 3rd of the line held by the 20th Brigade."[10] Accompanied by General Wu Chang Chi and his staff, the foreign officers exited the mines promptly at dawn.

Tick tock talk and tea, and General Chen and his entourage, plus Kuo and Sun returned to the hills to oversee the signing of the muster list. After hardy thanks and gracias, Eddie Elias, without his still captive brother Fred, Jerome Henley, Manuel Verea, and the now bandaged Theo Saphiere, were shuttled down the tracks to Lincheng and points beyond.

Coolies and couriers brought bad, then worse, news to the mines. The devil flying-machines and the foreign armies had panicked the bandits, who'd rushed their hostages to the mountain's summit. There'd been a scuffle, shots were fired, and one or more of the foreigners had been savagely slain! So tragic, just when everything was going so well, but just a rumor and not true.

The Military Commission returned to the mines around dinner time, and informed their respective consuls of the "total inadequacy of the pseudo-cordon and . . . that even this ridiculously weak line . . . was only a maneuver of the day, posted entirely for the benefit of the Commission."[11]

>Following from the Consul General, Tsinanfu dated Tsaochuang June 3rd.
>
>"British captives request that the following telegram be sent to His Majesty the King. Begins:
>
>'Remaining two British captives of Lincheng brigands offer respectfully birthday congratulations and petition for increased efforts to effect release.
>
>Elias and Rowlatt' "[12]

June 4

At about 9:00 A.M., the Military Commission set out on a second, shorter inspection of the Chinese troops. The officers were back by lunch time, having again witnessed scraggly lines and shabby military dramatics.

A letter from Musso and one from Powell confirmed that there was trouble with the food. Was it being sent? For a day, then two, they'd eaten rice twice thrice rice with rice for dessert. Yes, it was being sent.

After hearing evidence from the guards, crew, and riders of the #2 Up Train, the Joint Inquiry issued its rather narrow report. For reasons of health, including a desire not to be murdered, the Chinese delegates would not voice any criticism of their military superiors. B. G. Tours, John K. Davis, P. Crepin and Ferraiolo—representing Great Britain, the United States, France, and Italy—resolved to continue their investigation and produce a more comprehensive document.

In Peking: yet another political crisis. A tax called the "Hatamen Octroi" had long paid the police and maintained the city's schools and the presidential palace. Tsao Kun thought that this money could be better spent on Christian General Feng's unpaid troops. Pressure was applied to the cabinet, which issued papers appointing a new tax collector, one of Feng's men. But President Li wouldn't affix his seal and scolded the cabinet. The Premier quit, but his verbal resignation wasn't accepted. Mediators were brought in, but they now bailed out, viewing the situation as beyond repair.

June 5

Unfortunately for the captives, many of their immediate guards were of the hardened criminal type. Some of these rogues were now unearthing their booty, shedding some weaponry, and slipping out of the hills, "their departure presumably being winked at."[13] With their gradual disappearance, new, more soldierly guards came up to the temples, and the foreign food once again began arriving, bringing a welcome boost to sagging morale. Even Commodore Musso was feeling good enough to take a little stroll with a stick.

At the now daily meeting between the outlaw leaders and the government team, the chieftain demanded firm guarantees for the regular payment of their wages, and Roy Anderson said that he would telegraph Tsao Kun and see. . . .

Having seen quite enough Chinese army theatrical improvisations, the International Military Commission began packing their bags. Colonel J. M. Wainwright left the mines early to report to Minister Schurman.

In an animated discussion with Peking's witty wordsmith and reporter, Rodney Gilbert, a still high-strung Jerome Henley said that the whole escapade was political in nature, aimed at discrediting Tsao Kun. Roy Anderson, S. T. Wen, and the bilingual Chinese captives had all behaved magnificently. Any one of the foreigners could have easily escaped, but they all knew that this would make it worse for the others, so, said Henley, they stayed.

Ministers Plentipotentiary Sir Ronald Macleay and Jacob Gould Schurman were meanwhile discussing China's Railway Police. Not only did the local warlords whimsically interrupt service to shift their armies to and fro, but the physical possession of a railroad was the next best source of booty to controlling Peking. British investors had shoveled mounds of pounds into the railroads, and these massive loans were defaulting. After the wrecking of the Blue Express, foreigners of all nationalities were united in demanding that the rails be made safe.

June 6

In the morning, while the military registration was continuing in the hills, four bandit chiefs came to the more tranquil mines to smooth out further details.

> The bandits are quite at home at Tsaochuang now, and whereas it was at first difficult to induce them to allow a photograph to be taken, they are ready to submit to the attentions of as many cameras as can be brought to bear upon them. They will raise their hats, gently sway their fans, and smile broadly in the most approved movie manner.[14]

Barter and banter for several hours, then the honorable hill people were escorted into town for a little shopping.

> The local shopkeepers have incidentally been successful in doing a little polite banditry, though as the gentlemen from Paotzeku were using stolen money, they can hardly be said to be losers.[15]

Premier Chang Shao-tseng now tendered his resignation in writing. "The whole cabinet promptly resigned, on the pretext that the President had refused to dismiss the Chief of the Octroi."¹⁶ Like magic, Christian General Feng's orchestrated troops, plus local police, suddenly appeared outside the presidential palace demanding their wages. Come dark, ex-premier Chang and his family left—"fled"—the northern capital.

In the "Mountains Where the Bandits Live," there was great celebration, totally unrelated to the political chaos sweeping Peking, the news of which had not yet arrived. However, a good quantity of strong wine had. Sweet pipes were filled and filled again with opium, and random, pointless deathless shots were fired as a gay, drugged, and drunken mob invaded the Temples Among the Clouds, "causing much alarm."¹⁷

June 7

Half a world away, where it was still June 6th, serious questions were raised in the British Parliament concerning the fate of the captured British subjects and the "interest on loans made in good faith by investors in this country."¹⁸

In penniless Peking, President Li called Dr.'s W. W. Yen and V. K. W. Koo and other parliamentarians to the palace to try to enlist them in a new cabinet. These gentlemen were interested but cautious. Following this chat, Dr. Koo headed for a luncheon date with Dr. Schurman.

The International Military Commission now returned to the capital, and the officers dispersed to their respective legations to begin circulating their report. The Chinese authorities had said that approximately seven thousand loyal soldiers were stationed around the Cloud Nest Shrines. The foreign officers thought four thousand a more realistic figure. Of this number, "at least two brigades" were picking up pocket money by "selling arms and ammunition"[19] to the bandits.

After six days and nights on scenic Mount Pao Tzu Ku, Father Auguste Potte came down to the colliery and "gave a rather pessimistic view of the captives' lot."[20] Musso, Solomon, and Friedman had all had bouts with malaria. It was ghastly hot. Bugs everywhere. More than a few of the outlaws were suffering with dysentery, and at least two had leprosy. The foreigners were using disinfectant, but. . . . The only bright spot was that, during their explorations, the captives had fumbled onto a forgotten waterhole, a bathing hole. But tempers were snapping. Two guards had gotten into a fight over nothing-or-other, and one of them bit off the end of the other's finger. Powell rubbed one of the outlaws wrong, and the rogue shoved him. But Powell replied with flying fists and pummeled the man into medical attention!

Attending to matters of state, Li Yuan-hung invited more guests to the palace, and the lights burned late as the president tried to pull a new cabinet out of his magic hat.

June 8

General Wang, Tsao Chwang.

Please decode the following telegram and forward same to Mr. Anderson:

International Pressure 155

"Mr. Anderson:

You have acted as a negotiator in the Lincheng bandit case and, in spite of the hot weather and hardships, have exerted your full energy as a mediator. I greatly appreciate this. As the case has now been discussed and a solution has been found, please do not hesitate to give the several guarantees demanded by the bandits, in order that both Chinese and foreign captives may be relieved from danger at an early date. I greatly hope that the case will now be settled in this manner. I therefore send you this telegram, trusting that you will note the same.

Tsao Kun [seal]"[21]

Hours before this message would find Anderson, a special train slipped into the mines bringing uniforms and dollars.

Li Yuan-hung's efforts to "form a new cabinet under Dr. Wellington Koo or Dr. W. W. Yen received no encouragement from the legislators,"[22] and some discouragement from the tuchuns, gangsters, and warlords.

By order of the police chiefs, Tsao Kun men, the Peking police, numbering between 4,000 and 5,000 men, went on strike June 9 at 6 a.m.[23]

The Minister in China to the Secretary of State

Peking, June 9, 1923 — 10 a.m.

Peking police quit at 6 o'clock this morning. Members of my staff, civil and military, have been going about ever

156   *Outrage at Lincheng*

since and report everything quiet and shops open. General Munthe's Legation Quarter force of four companies remain on duty. . . . I will promptly telegraph any new developments. Although no danger to foreigners is apprehended, I am watching the situation closely and already had a consultation with military members of my staff. . . .

Schurman[24]

During the day a coolie demonstration, led by police and gendarmes in plain clothes, and paid so many coppers a head by Tsao Kun campaign leaders, made a demonstration before the President's house wither he had moved in the morning because the Palace guards had been withdrawn.[25]

Gram for Mr. Anderson. Decoded telegram for Mr. Anderson. Decoded tele. . . .

Minister in China to the Secretary of State

Peking, June 9, 1923 — 8 p.m.

Strike ended. Reasons obscure. No change in Peking. Koo has informed me that he has requested President to drop his name from further consideration for premiership.

Schurman[26]

June 10

Following a conference with General Conner, Dr. Schurman cabled Washington his recommendation that "the

International Pressure 157

3rd battalion of the 15th Infantry should be sent to Tientsin from the Philippines as a gesture of respect to the Lincheng affair."[27] Besieged at his own home by plainclothes police, President Li said that he would not be intimidated and launched several telegrams to his friends in the provinces.

Underpaid and underfed, some of the provincial troops surrounding Pao Tzu Ku were restless and perhaps curious about just how much silver the foreign devils would fetch. Although not openly mutinous, the troops aroused concerns that there might be "disturbances."

Negotiations All But Complete

Tsaochuang, June 10

Two bandit representatives left Tsaochuang yesterday and returned this morning with General Chen. It is stated that the negotiations should be completed today and that General Chen believes that the captives will be released tomorrow.

All the Chinese officials and Mr. Anderson have been invited to the Bandit camp tomorrow. It is believed that the usual Chinese celebration is to be held at the completion of the negotiations.

It is stated that Mr. Anderson will be asked to act as guarantor for the agreement and that the Chinese Chamber of Commerce and the Shantung gentry delegates will arrange for the release of the Chinese prisoners.[28]

Peking's Ministry of Communications held up President Li's telegrams. The lights may have burned late at the president's home, but someone had cut the water and telephone lines.

June 11

In London, under-secretary of state for foreign affairs, Mr. Ronald McNeill, stated that "His Majesty's Minister at Pekin has been authorized to press for the establishment of a railway police force under foreign officers."[29]

In Beijing, the Diplomatic Corps met and met again as the day progressed. A certain comfort in numbers? If there were war between the Chihli and Manchurian forces.... The diplomats traded some sweet-talk about "Allied" troop strength in China's future, present and Boxer past, but there was business to attend to. All indications were that the captives would momentarily be freed, so a committee was appointed to determine what guarantees and sanctions to demand from the Chinese government.

Dusk. Sun Mei-yao and several aides hiked up to the temples, called the captives together, and announced that it was now definite that the Honorable Mr. Roy Anderson, Esq., would come to the chiefs' village on the morrow.

This news stirred only "mild interest" among the foreigners, who'd been hearing a similar promise for days. However, the hostages replied that their representatives would be ready. One chief suggested that it might be nice if Mr. Anderson enjoyed the chiefs' hospitality for a couple of weeks, or a moon. The prisoners protested, words flowed, and dusk slipped into dark. The path down would be difficult

International Pressure 159

and could be treacherous, so Sun Mei-yao and staff joined the captives for a snooze among the shrines.

June 12

Sun up, and the captives were awake, in good spirits, and making bets among themselves as to whether or not they'd be freed today. According to their hosts, Mr. Anderson was due at the chiefs' headquarters at 9:00 A.M., so there was time for tea. At 8:00 A.M., Powell and Solomon, representing the captives, and Dr. Hung, translator and Chinese representative, headed down the stairs, through the woods, past the first outpost, two or three tricky mulepath miles to Shih Li Ho, the Ten Li River. More of a creek. And the village wasn't much either: a few scrawny adobe huts quite deep in outlaw turf. Lots of guards about. And bossmen, chiefs, dozens of hardened men with other encampments nearby. Roy Anderson did not arrive at 9:00 A.M., although more chiefs did. Mr. Anderson did not arrive at ten, eleven, twelve, or thirteen, although more rogues and rumors did.

"Generals Feng Yu-hsiang, the Christian General, and General Wang Hsai-ching, who between them control all the troops about Peking, sent the President their resignations."[30] The advice reaching His Excellency President Li was: flee.

Two in the afternoon, and relayed signals arrived from lookouts. Horsemen were coming. Coolies shouldering a chair headed a long train of sedan chairs with more and more cavalry. One hundred mounted men and a score of borne leaders plus their bearers. Solomon and Powell plowed into this intricate entourage, and found Anderson's conveyance. They told Roy that the bandits might want him to stay, but that he should not. They also informed Anderson that the chiefs wanted all documents to be stamped with some imaginary foreign seal.

Groups of guests were escorted into a baked mud shed with thatched roof, some twenty feet long, ten feet wide, eight feet high. One room, no windows, dark, stale, stark, one door. Anderson and Wen entered, the latter seating himself at a table in the center. Anderson circulated in the smoky semi-dark, as did General Chen Tiao-yuan and General Wu, with bodyguards and aides-de-camp.

Anderson found old Bo-bo Liu and the younger Sun Mei-yao and bluntly upbraided them for adding last-minute demands, of which both men denied all knowledge. Roy put on the jacket he'd only moments ago removed and walked out in a show of leaving, or perhaps for some wise last air.

The most venerable Sung Kwei-chi, aged, former member of the gentry and chief-of-chiefs, played the diplomat as more literati, gentry, soldiers, and nearly soldiers crowded into the long room. Opium was cooking in the corners and the air soon became thick, sweet, and warm. The room became overcrowded and, while gossip and banter flowed freely, soldiers and gentry took their turns at these corner peace pipes. Yes, the uniforms and silver were coming, but the carts were heavy and had to go slow in the hills. Mr. Kiang Chin-yuan, of the Commercial Guild of Peking— perhaps you know my esteemed father's second cousin?

Foreign affairs specialist S. T. Wen, unfurled and began reading aloud from an unsigned Chinese document.

June 1923

To: The Most Honourable Chief Sung
and all other Chiefs.

I, Roy S. Anderson, am an American citizen and a friend of China in life and death. As the brethren in the mountains are having hard times, as all Tan Chai [chiefs] have shown genuine sincerity in their actions and words in all the conferences, and as they are willing to submit, I am willing to guarantee that my brethren will be organized into an army and made officers and privates. There shall be no more than three thousand people and the number of unarmed men shall not exceed five hundred. The Government will undertake to support two thousand and seven hundred people while all Tan Chai [chiefs] shall make arrangements to pay the three hundred men, themselves. I am also willing to guarantee that after the brethren are "called and pacified," all their former crimes will be pardoned by the Government. After they are organized, their pay as agreed upon will be given to them according to their ranks, every month, by the Government. This guarantee shall be effective three years from the date of signing.

After you, my brethren, have submitted, you shall, for the sake of your country and fellow citizens, be loyal to your country and keep the order of the army, so that the whole nation, seeing that you are serving the country, will praise your spirit of sacrifice.[31]

Old Chief Sung now unveiled his own parchment, praised the gentlemen present and the ancestors past, and announced that he was ready to sign, saying, "I am going to use my new army for the defence of the Republic of China!"[32]

Someone applauded, then everyone applauded as Sung affixed his name and seal. Several local gentry stepped forward to witness Chief Sung's pledge, to more applause and encouraging words. A good-natured game of musical chairs followed as Roy Anderson formally signed his guarantee, and the Chinese literati affixed their names in witness and moved to likewise sign below Chief Sung's words. Then came the most applause of all as the carts bringing the uniforms and boxes of silver arrived!

June, 1923

To: Mr. Anderson.

I, Sung Kwei-chi, representing all brethren here, beg to say that we are willing to be "callcd and pacified" and organized into a national army. From this time on, we will be permanently loyal to the country and commit nothing that will disturb the order of the army or hurt the reputation of soldiers. On behalf of all brethren, I beg to make this important declaration that we have full confidence in Mr. Anderson and to the person of Mr. Anderson we pledge that we will permanently observe the above things.

Sung Kwei-chi
Hsin [faith]

Witness:

    Kiang Chin-yuan
    Sung Fu-chi
    Chou Sih-sung
    Pao Wei-er
    [etc.][33]

International Pressure 163

Men came and went from the hut. The several foreigners took turns stepping out for a breather, but returned to the suffocating room where the ceremony of signing was winding down.

S. T. Wen asked, then pressed for the release of the eight remaining foreign captives as well as three named Chinese who'd acted as their cooks, helpers, interpreters. The chiefs hedged a bit, but one man finally scribbled something and handed the note to an aide. Lee Solomon latched onto this chap and hurried him out the door.

The path led mostly uphill. The happy hurry was slowed by the grade and the tricks in the path, but Solomon pushed himself and prodded the bandit. They climbed, scrambled, and ran up the hills, into and through the bandit village, up into the arbor, past the tiny, ceaseless spring, up the old chiseled steps, huffing and puffing through the arch of honor and into the cluster of temples. Solomon was all winded, panting, shouting: "Free, free!"[34]

The remaining "Old Guard," as the last eight foreigners had come to be called in the newspapers, hadn't necessarily believed, but they'd picked and packed, and the bilinguals were ready, so off in a dash, their guards pouncing on the abandoned gear. Down they pranced from the Cloud Nest Temples on the Calf in Hand Mountain in the Pao Tu Shan!

There was still much business to attend to at the Ten Li River. The local gentry were arranging the release of "twenty odd Chinese passengers," and there were more additions to the muster list, plus clarifications and instructions, uniforms, and the fifty or was it eighty-five thousand silver dollars. Bobo Liu was still not happy, still conspiring at 4:30 P.M. when the captives assembled at Shih Li Ho, ready for the jaunt to the mines, ready and eager, but the new army wasn't.

Chief and/or Brigadier General Sun Mei-yao's "honored guests" deserved a special Guard-of-Honor, and twenty-five new soldiers in new uniforms would soon be ready. A slight delay then, as the donkeys, coolies, palanquins, and a cavalry escort were readied.

Good cloth was dear, so the new recruits popped their army caps atop their straw hats and pulled their uniforms on over their ragamuffin garb, which dangled forth. Then to the asses, chairs, footpaths and mines: Forward Ho!

Several li ahead was no man's land, but before they could reach it, an outlaw came up fast from behind and stopped the bizarre caravan. All Chinese captives except Dr. Hung must return! The agreement was for three Chinese! Five had come! Four must go back, but Chi Cheng broke and ran, and another student snatched a soldier's horse and fled, but two other Chinese were seized and taken back!

A somber li or three, nearing the contested land, the motley outlaw escort mostly just melted away. All except "Ivan" alias "Rusky," the coolie who'd fought with the Bolsheviks in Siberia but who had served Lee Solomon faithfully and now, via private arrangement, was traveling under Mr. Solomon's protection. Soon government troops, and more troops as the party rode and trudged on to the general's field headquarters, where reporters and Pathé men pounced. A pleasant delay, then into the yamen for a toast with "three treasured bottles of Champagne."[35] Then back to the awkward chairs and donkeys, although some foreigners preferred to stretch their legs, but not Musso. With light fading, into the colliery and a massive explosion of warmth and welcome!

It was past the pampered gentlemen's bedtime, about 4:00 A.M., when two small trains left the mines. One, with Major Pinger, Reginal Rowlatt, and some consular staff, headed north. The other, carrying the rest of the sleeping Old Guard Captives' Club—Powell, Solomon, Leon Friedman, Emile Gensburger, Fred Elias, and the slimmer Musso— chugged for Shanghai.

June 13

The representatives of the United States, Great Britain, France, Italy, Belgium, the Netherlands, and Japan met in committee and readily agreed that the newly freed hostages deserved compensation for their ordeal. But the committee could not immediately agree on how large an indemnity, or how to reorganize the railway police, or what guarantees to demand from the Chinese government.

President Li set his hand to several special mandates. He accepted the premier's and cabinet's resignations. He appointed a new premier and minister of war. Finally, he "abolished the post of all the tuchuns and made all the units of the army directly responsible to the Ministry of War."[36] Li forwarded these documents to the Government Printing Office, which "refused to accept them."[37] After entrusting the presidential seal to one of his concubines—known in the Victorian press as "his wife"—Li Yuan-hung boarded his special train and headed south.

CAPTIVES ARRIVAL AT SHANGHAI

The largest crowd that has ever met a train in Shanghai gathered at the Shanghai North Station on Wednesday night to welcome the Lincheng captives. When the train drew under the sheds, cheer upon cheer rose in salvoes and, as it came to a slow speed the Russian Cadet Band, brought there because two Shanghai men thought that the reception should lack nothing, broke into "See the Conquering Hero Comes". Then pandemonium broke loose, there was a grand rush of wives and daughters and the bearded men were almost thrown to the ground under the impetus of the greetings and kisses they received. A moment's pause until each man was identified, then followed individual cheers for him. Hats were thrown into the air and men cheered themselves hoarse, while tears streamed down the cheeks of those near and dear.[38]

Looking "hale and cheerful," big Leon Friedman was the only shaved captive. "He said that the bandits feared him, probably because of his size."

"Mr. J. B. Powell's beard was much sturdier than most of the returned captives. He looked like a leader among ancient Russian revolutionists, in the days before they became prosperous. Mr. Powell looked older and weary."

"Commander G. D. Musso looked old, worn and very ill. He had to carry crutches and was suffering. While the mob cheered as they were momentarily halted, the captives were raised to the shoulders of their friends, and as dozens of magnesium sticks were lighted, the motion-picture camera registered every move."[39]

"In this way the Lincheng incident, which had caused such a sensation both home and abroad, was brought to a close."[40]

The Outrage at Lincheng, which has deeply stirred the foreign communities here, is but one manifestation of underlying chaotic conditions liable to produce similar phenomena of greater extent and much more serious and fatal results at any time.[41]

Jacob Gould Schurman

34. Tientsin Pukow engine (Courtesy of AlCo Historic Photos). This luxurious Blue Train was built by American Car & Foundry in 1922 and had only been in service for several months when the bandits demolished it. The locomotive was a light 4-6-2 Pacific built by AlCo - Schenectady in 1920.

35. Relief car (Courtesy of The Joint Collection, University of Missouri).

36. John K. Davis (Courtesy of The Joint Collection, University of Missouri).

37. Sleeping compartments and the Drawing Room (Courtesy of American Car & Foundry).

38. Private car (Courtesy of American Car & Foundry).

Chapter Twelve

LINCHENG COMMITTEE

President Li's train received a special welcome at Tientsin's Central Station: General Wang's troops surrounded it and, "for about twelve hours," held the president captive.[1] The price for allowing Li Yuan-hung sanctuary in the British concession was his written resignation plus the seals of office. Only after Peking confirmed that Li's wife had indeed given up the seals was his ex-excellency allowed to slip away into the 4:00 A.M. darkness, June 14.

In London, where it was still June 13th,

> Sir A. Holbrook asked the Under-Secretary of State for Foreign Affairs whether he is aware that the recent outrage

on the Tientsin-Pukow Railway has shown that travel outside the Treaty Ports in China is increasingly unsafe, and that unless drastic action is taken promptly trade in China will soon be impossible; and what steps the British Government propose to take to secure the lives of British subjects there?[2]

His Majesty's representative in China, Sir Ronald Macleay, was considering "requesting his government to bring the British force up to its prewar strength."[3] Indeed, talk of calling in reinforcements seems to have dominated a discussion between the British, American, French, and Japanese ministers.

As for the Chinese government, that is, the "internationally recognized" government of the Republic of China, that is, the northern government of the city-state of Peking. . . . The president was gone. There was no premier, no vice-president, and the entire cabinet had resigned. But, ignoring their own exit-visas, several cabinet ministers assembled to try to carry on "pending further developments."[4]

June 15

The Lincheng Committee met again and decided, in their tentative communiqué, to inform the Chinese Government that they were activating a dormant "Boxer Protocol," and would send observers into the provinces to monitor bandit activity and to oversee the officials responsible for maintaining order. Any mandarins not protecting foreigners would be summarily punished. The committee also decided to press for the settlement of several long-standing issues, including the improvement of Shanghai's harbor and "the extension of the International Settlement." Although the ambassadors again agreed that China's railroad police needed revamping, they still couldn't agree on the details. Sir Ronald was advocating an extensive reorganization of the rails using foreign troops. The chargé d'affaires for Japan "said his government, while favoring an effective police force, was opposed to foreign management.... It was generally felt that the terms which the Commission recommended for the settlement of the Lincheng outrage would not be accepted by the Chinese Government."[5]

The plentipotentiaries of the United States and Great Britain "walked homeward together." Macleay thought that, even though the Japanese were initially unresponsive to the idea, they "would join if British and American warships made a demonstration." But Dr. Schurman said he thought his government "would be opposed to using force." Schurman also believed it possible to "use the present political crisis to advantage," but he didn't share these thoughts with his colleague.[6]

"My life was repeatedly threatened especially by well-armed but irresponsible boy-bandits," Roland Pinger testified in an affidavit given to consul staff. "At all times, for the sake of my family, I tried to send only cheerful news...."[7]

Jerome Henley had also hidden the truth:

> On two occasions when I did something that displeased my guards, two or three of them covered me with rifles and

revolvers while one of them severely beat me with a club. Also on several occasions my guards pointed rifles at me and threatened to shoot me. One day one of the Chinese Captains told me that one of my guards, who had taken a dislike to me, said he was going to shoot me some night. Three or four nights after hearing this I lay awake in agony and fear that I would be shot.[8]

The committee met again on June 18, and settled the question of compensation "for the loss of liberty and moral and physical sufferings and hardships endured by the foreigners."[9] For their first three days, when the hostages were herded along in horrible marches, they should each receive five hundred dollars per day—enough to buy two or three Model T's. For each subsequent day, they were to receive one hundred dollars, enough to buy a dromedary or two, although not the "One Hundred Thousand Gold Dollars" Jerome Henley was demanding.

The following day, to the sound of one hand clapping, Li Yuan-hung "revoked" his resignation. Meanwhile, in Washington, the British Embassy gave the American State Department a memo commending Sir Ronald's railway scheme but warning that there would be difficulty "in securing its acceptance by China unless the Powers present a united front."[10]

In Peking, the representatives of Japan, the United States, Great Britain, France, Italy, Belgium, and the Netherlands, alias the Lincheng Committee, agreed on June 20 that those to be dismissed and forever excluded from similar office included: (1) Shantung's military governor, Tien Chung-yu; (2) General Ho Feng-yu, the truculent boss of the mines and the Lincheng district; (3) The commander of the Tientsin-Pukow Railway police; and (4) Chao, the officer in immediate command of the guard on the wrecked train.[11]

The Minister in China to the Secretary of State
Peking, June 22, 1923—10:00 a.m.

For exemplary and punitive damages suffered by himself and family in Lincheng Outrage, Major Allen has presented claim of $50,000 gold and Major Pinger $60,000. I am informed that Shanghai victims of the outrage are presenting still larger claims.

Schurman[12]

The Lincheng Committee had, by June 22, completed a tentative draft of their definitive "Note." However, the ambassadors felt they shouldn't present it to Peking's full Diplomatic Corps "until we have heard from our Governments what measures they will authorize for the enforcement of the terms of settlement proposed by the committee in the event of the Chinese Government proving recalcitrant."[13]

Clarifications soon arrived. Secretary Hughes wired Schurman his pronouncement that the final communiqué not include any obviously unrelated demands, such as the improvement of Shanghai's harbor. While Hughes thought that a foreign controlled railroad police might be "meritorious," the U.S. would not support such a plan if it were engineered "for the rehabilitation of British railway loans."[14] Nor was Hughes enthusiastic about demonstrating allied military might.

Lincheng Committee 173

"Brigadier General" Sun Mei-yao's newly reorganized "regiment" now marched away from the Buddhist monastery where they'd been trapped since spring. A second "regiment," slower to get it together, remained encamped in and around the Temples Among the Clouds.

Before the end of June, Tsao and his agents had elicited telegrams from every tuchun and provincial official of any influence, with the single exception of Wu Pei-fu, Tsao's military mainstay, exhorting Parliament to elect Tsao Kun President. Meanwhile more and more members of Parliament began to desert the Capital.[15]

On June 30, the British Embassy handed the United States State Department another communiqué. His Majesty's government agreed that the Shanghai questions "should be omitted as being irrelevant." But the British representative stressed that, if the United States, Great Britain, and Japan would act in unison, "the Chinese will yield long before it becomes necessary to exercise coercion."[16]

The Chinese General Chamber of Commerce has sent a further telegram to the Military and Civil Governors of Shantung demanding instant action to effect the release of the wretched Chinese still captive at Paotzeku. We have already once called attention to the derelict state of these poor people and their pathetic message cannot be forgotten: "Now that the foreigners have been let go," they wrote, "nobody bothers any more about us."[17]

July 2

On July 2, in London, more probing questions concerning the chaos sweeping China resounded in the House of Commons. But in Tokyo, Britain's call for vigorous action met with a parry. The British Chargé d'affaires "reported that the head of the Asiatic Department . . . was sceptical about the effectiveness of a Naval demonstration. . . ." and that "the Japanese government seemed . . . considerably surprised by the strong measures Britain had proposed."[18]

A week later, Secretary Hughes informed the British Embassy that the American government also doubted the value of a nebulous naval parade. Instead, Hughes sounded out the British about the "withholding of recognition from any new Government that may seek to assume power in the present political crisis."[19] This "nonrecognition" would mean that the Western powers wouldn't fork over any revenue from the "Chinese" Maritime Customs. Without this money, the Peking Government couldn't function.

In Canton, Dr. Sun Yat-sen called upon the Western nations to finally dump Peking's parody of a democracy. In Shanghai, supporters of his Ex-excellency Li Yuan-hung were rallying and trying to form a new legislature. Peking's parliamentarians found they could do some lucrative commuting.

> It became a contest between Tsao Kun, who spent money to keep them in Peking, and the Central China Movement, also spending money to effect the assembly of Parliament in Shanghai. By taking pleasant trips to and fro . . .

these venal solons received pay from both sources and fattened while they traveled.[20]

On July 16, the Lincheng Committee completed drafting its Joint Communiqué with a last minute decision to jack up the cash indemnities they would demand on behalf of the hostages. But the Japanese, French, and American representatives still had differing thoughts concerning China's Railway Police. Since Sir Ronald Macleay was away, the committee postponed action.

Since he was already unofficially acting as foreign minister, on July 23rd, Dr. V. K. Wellington Koo "took office as Minister of Foreign Affairs under an assurance from all parties . . . that he would not be called upon to participate in any way in politics but would function simply as a go-between in the settlement of China's many misunderstandings with the Powers."[21]

Vacationing from the rigors of state by enjoying an Alaskan cruise, W. Gamaliel Harding ate some spoiled crab and returned to a hospital in San Francisco. Pneumonia was followed by real progress, but then came an unexpected stroke. On August 2, President Harding died, and the United States plunged into mourning and tributes for Warren G. who'd been well-liked. Even though there were rumbles, the Teapot Dome scandals hadn't yet exploded. Nor did anyone speak openly of suicide, jealousy, or poisons other than ptomaine. American foreign policy was not affected.

On August 10, after a review by Peking's full Diplomatic Corps, the Lincheng Note was formally presented to Dr. Koo. Koo immediately summoned a special committee with delegates from the Ministry of Communications, the Army, Internal Affairs, Foreign Affairs, and Finance. These gentlemen went to work assembling ideas, rebuttals, and responses. Within three days, a reply was ready. Like a true diplomat, Dr. Koo tucked his answer up his sleeve.

The newspapers were quick to publish and pick apart the "Note of the Sixteen Nations." According to the foreign and Chinese tabloids, the Lincheng Note was: (A) too mild; (B) too harsh; (C) too late; (D) about right; (E) all of the above. But in the Chinese press, a growing storm of protest raged.[22]

Peking, Aug. 17

Dr. Wellington Koo replying to questions by correspondents, today said that the Government would do its utmost to expedite a reply.[23]

Because of absences, disagreements, and the complexity of trying to reorganize China's railroad guards, Peking's Diplomatic Corps had merely "reserved the right, after a more considered study of the questions, to present their scheme when elaborated to the Chinese Government."[24] On August 20, the committee finally debated Ambassador Macleay's proposals.

Tough and far reaching, the British plan placed China's railway police and revenues under foreign control for a period of not less than ten years. Sir Ronald's scheme was unanimously adopted "after amendment."[25] As originally proposed, this new Railway Defence Bureau was to have "a foreign officer as its chief,"[26] but due to Japanese pressure

Lincheng Committee 177

and the reluctance of the American Minister, the foreigner's job title became that of "associate director."[27] The Chinese police had at first been conceived of as being under foreign military command, but the foreign officers' roles shrank to that of "instructors and inspectors." But the revenues would receive careful scrutiny from "foreign chief accountants."[28] To "maintain a united policy among the Powers,"[29] Britain had compromised. The Japanese minister approved the revised scheme, "subject to instructions from his Government."[30]

Physician, revolutionary, and retroactive statesman, Sun Yat-sen had issued a manifesto that expertly tied Peking's warlords to the Lincheng mess, and Dr. Sun continued to press the foreign powers to withdraw their "recognition" from the moribund regime. But Sun Yat-sen had been asking the Allied democracies to recognize his southern republic for years to no avail. Lately, a newly flexing Soviet Union was showing some interest, so, before the month was out, Sun sent one of his lieutenants to Russia on educational leave. It was Chiang Kai-shek who went to Moscow, not Mao. Mao was in Shanghai implementing an alliance between the small Communist party and Dr. Sun's larger Kuomintang—the Nationalists. "If one of our foreign masters farts," Mao Tse Tung joked in August, "it's a lovely perfume."[31]

> While waiting for the Chinese reply to the Lincheng demands, Schurman continued to see Foreign Minister Koo. On August 29, and again on September 21, Schurman urged Koo to give a prompt reply to the Diplomatic Corps.[32]

On September 1, part of the Pacific "rim of fire" quaked; Tokyo fell down and burned. Massive devastation. 240,000 dead. Communications were shattered, and Japan's foreign policy *was* effected as Japanese at home and abroad looked to and for their families.

In southern Shantung and elsewhere, the sorghum crop—the hardy stalks of kaoliang—now stood six to ten feet tall, perfect for hiding bandits. In Shantung province and elsewhere, Governor Tien Chung-yu, whom the foreigners wanted ousted, was still finding supporters.

On September 9, former President Li Yuan-hung left the British Concession in Tientsin and detrained at Shanghai to test the political waters. They weren't warm.

>The presidential election was set for September 12. Elaborate preparations were made, and by order of the police, Peking was decorated from end to end with flags, but Parliament could not assemble a quorum and there was no election. During the next few weeks, preparations were made for the bribery of Parliament on a huge scale.[33]

>The reply of the Chinese Government to the "Lincheng Note" of the Powers was a carefully worded statement. Foreign Minister Koo refuted the basis of each item of the Diplomatic Corps' demands.[34]

Koo informed the honorable ministers that the Chinese government was "impressed" because the Lincheng Note had been "signed by all the Chiefs of Missions of the Diplomatic Body including those Powers whose nationals were happily not found among the victims of the unfortunate incident."[35] Dr. Koo stated that "although several months have elapsed since the incident took place, time has not mitigated the sense of outrage with which the Chinese Government review it." However, "careful consideration of the facts of the case leads us to the conclusion that no liability for damages can be predicated on the Chinese Government." Nonetheless, the Chinese would accept "the three categories of damages A.B. and C. outlined in Your Excellency's Note," but not the supplementary claims. As to the reorganization of China's railway police, this was "an urgent problem of China's internal administration." But Dr. Koo closed on a hopeful note:

> The Chinese Government trust that through the series of new measures which they have recently adopted . . . the lives, the property, the rights and interests of foreigners in China will be able to enjoy added security throughout the country.
> I have the honor to add that an identical communication is being addressed to the other Chiefs of Missions who are signatories of the Note under reply.[36]

The North China *Herald* found Dr. Koo's communiqué less than adequate:

> Nirvana.
>
> Not till September 24 did Dr. Wellington Koo trouble himself to reply—then with an answer of smooth evasion and hardly veiled insolence.[37]

180 *Outrage at Lincheng*

The "Chiefs of Missions," who may have preferred to think of themselves as "plentipotentiaries," met on September 27 and considered Dr. Koo's reply. "Sentiment was unanimous against modifying any part of the demands."[38] However, the ambassadors were not immediately clear on how to proceed, and they decided to address Koo's note at their next meeting.

On October 1-3, the full Diplomatic Corps and the smaller Lincheng Committee debated and completed their response to Dr. Koo's reply.

> The diplomatic body had hoped that following this incident the Chinese Government would inaugurate vigorous actions against the brigands who infest the country. . . . It is not enough to give an order to pursue the brigands . . . it is necessary that the brigands actually be pursued. . . .
>
> Under these conditions the diplomatic body . . . find themselves compelled to maintain in their entirety the considerations and conclusions of their collective note of August 10th last.[39]

The ambassadors now openly hinted that if the new Chinese government balked at these demands, they would put into effect a policy of "nonrecognition."

On October 5, Peking's Parliament elected Tsao Kun president. Tsao received 480 votes, 37 more than needed. The going price per vote was $5,000, although congressional "whips" got $10,000 each, for a super deluxe total that ran into the millions. Tsao Kun's other qualifications included being primitive, uncultured, and having once, a decade earlier, sacked the northern capital. Dr. Schurman reported "No enthusiasm, no crowds, only police, soldiers and rickshaw men in the streets."[40] In Canton, Dr. Sun Yat-sen declared paper-tiger war against the new president and called upon various leaders to join with him in a Northern Punitive Expedition!

On October 10, the anniversary of the founding of the Republic, Tsao Kun was sworn in. Although invited to the ceremonies, none of the ambassadors attended.

The following day, Dr. Schurman informed Washington that "the diplomatic corps will not take part in official or social courtesies until the Chinese Government gives us assurances of compliance with the demands in the Lincheng notes. It is expected that these will be given within a few days."[41]

Indeed, Foreign Minister Koo and others came cooing, and an agreement was reached. Dr. Koo would, by the evening of the fourteenth, present the Diplomatic Body with another reply to the "Note of the Sixteen Nations." Koo's note, however, would be dated October 15, the very morning that the new President was planning to hold a reception. If Dr. Koo's reply was satisfactory, the foreign ambassadors would attend the function and trade diplomatic pleasantries.

Foreign Minister Koo, in writing, duly informed the diplomats that the Chinese government now agreed in principle to the supplementary claims earlier refused. The problem of tuchun Tien's dismissal had been a touchy one, but Koo stated that a presidential mandate of October 14 "relieved the said Military Governor of his post."

As for the railway police, Minister Koo again tried a dodge: "While the Chinese Government cannot commit themselves to the scheme or schemes which the Diplomatic

Body intends to present, they fully appreciate the interest which it takes in this problem. . . ."[42]

But this palaver didn't satisfy the diplomats, who demanded and received a verbal promise that the Chinese government would "receive and consider" the railway reorganization plan.

> The Foreign envoys in Peking attended the reception of President Tsao Kun at 11:00 a.m. on October 15. After a brief address by the President, they were all received and exchanged amenities with the new President of the "fictitious republic."[43]

Whatever goodwill Tsao Kun's reception generated lasted only one day. The next day, the government gazette published the latest decrees. Indeed, tuchun Tien had been removed from office, however the very next mandate promoted Tien to the rank of Marshal. The foreign community was "seething with indignation."[44] Dr. Koo and Dean De Freitas both threatened to resign. But the misunderstanding was quickly cleared up. A new mandate blossomed, explaining that the other two mandates had accidently been inverted in their order. Tien's promotion might thus be viewed as inoperative, "nugatory," worthless. Or it might not be, say what?

The *Atlantic Monthly* magazine, in its November offering, published a long letter that Lucy Aldrich had written earlier.

My Dear Sister,

> I suppose if I am ever going to write you about our adventure I'd better begin at once, as I am getting to the place

where I want to put the whole thing out of my mind, for a while at least. Of course, for the rest of my life, when I am "stalled" conversationally, it will be a wonderful thing to fall back on: "Oh, I must tell you about the time I was captured by Chinese bandits." That remark, from a fat, domestic-looking old lady in a Worth gown ought to wake up the dullest dinner party. . . .[45]

AMERICAN CONSULAR SERVICE

Tsinan, China, December 22, 1923

Subject: Execution of Sun Mei-yao.

The Honorable Jacob Gould Schurman,
American Minister
Peking China

Sir:
 I have the honor to report that Sun Mei-yao, the leader of the bandits responsible for the Lincheng hold-up this Spring, was executed on December 19, 1923. . . .[46]

 Swen Miao's band was surrounded by Chinese troops and he was captured and beheaded.[47]

 It was arranged between the Defence Commissioner and Colonel Wu to have Sun Mei-yao call for a conference at Wu's headquarters, which are in the mine compound at Tsaochuang. . . . Sun obeyed and he and his immediate bodyguard were shot. Later the company of about seventy men at Sun's headquarters were disarmed.[48]

184 Outrage at Lincheng

His followers were marched into an ambush and were disarmed and disbanded.[49]

The Governor of Shantung . . . massacred some six hundred of them with machine guns.[50]

This survey makes no attempt to go beyond 1923 because after that date the impact of Marxism-Leninism on Chinese thought and politics obviously becomes one of the central problems awaiting study, and it is treated by others elsewhere.[51]

The following claims in respect to the Lincheng outrage were handed in to the Chinese Government in April, 1924. . . . Grand Total 363.301.42.[52]

The Minister in China reported by telegram no. 75, February 23, 1925, the payment by the Chinese Government of $351,567.92 in full payment of Lincheng A and B claims to foreigners (file no 393.1123 Lincheng/294.) No payment was made on the supplementary claims which were presented.[53]

Nothing came of the Railway Reorganization Scheme.

The settlement of the Lincheng incident restored the relationship between the Chinese Government and the foreign representatives at Peking to one of mutual toleration. It did not, however, bring an end to banditry and anti-foreign incidents. . . .[54]

Reflecting upon this ordeal, journalist J. B. Powell recalled, "It was early spring and a bright moon was shining. . . ."[55]

Said *China Press* reporter, Lloyd Lehrbas, who also was kidnapped from the elegant Blue Express, "The night was very dark with hardly any moonlight. . . ."[56]

Appendix

A Week-End with Chinese Bandits

by Lucy Truman Aldrich

Peking, China
May 20, 1923

My Dear Sister,

I suppose if I am ever going to write you about our adventure I'd better begin at once, as I am getting to the place where I want to put the whole thing out of my mind, for a while at least. Of course, for the rest of my life, when I am 'stalled' conversationally, it will be a wonderful thing to fall back on: 'Oh, I must tell you about the time I was captured by Chinese bandits.' That remark, from a fat, domestic-looking old lady in a Worth gown, ought to wake up the dullest dinner party. I think I shall begin at the beginning and try to tell you everything as it happened.

We left Shanghai early Saturday morning, taking a Chinese guide with us as far as Nanking, where we changed for the Peking train. We had so much hand luggage with us, we were afraid of losing it on the ferry. With a good deal of bustle and rushing around, we finally settled down in two compartments on the Peking-Pukow express—Mathilde and I in one and Miss MacFadden in the other. The car was much the most luxurious I have ever seen in the East, quite the last thing in modern sleeping-cars, more like the Twentieth Century Limited than Chinese.

We had a very good dinner in an equally up-to-date dining car, and I amused myself watching—and criticizing, alas!—a party of young English in front of us. They were in their shirt sleeves and the table was piled with money. When they finished, the man who won jammed a big wad of bills into his pocket and strolled out of the car, jingling silver in both hands. Much good it did him!

I had given a small S. O. dinner party the night before and we were awfully tired, so decided to go to bed early. I went to sleep almost immediately and was aroused by the train stopping with a jerk. I got up, half asleep, put on a thin silk wrapper and bed-slippers, and without speaking to Mathilde, who was over my head, went into the corridor. Everything was quiet except for a (to me) queer crackling noise outside; but no one was in sight. I was just going to open the door and go back, when Miss MacFadden grabbed me, dragged me into her stateroom, slammed the door, and said in a queer breathless whisper, 'They are attacking the train and are just outside.' I peeked out through the curtain and saw a crowd of people. It was still dark and I could only see dimly, but they seemed to be swarming into the train. Miss MacFadden put her cape around me and her coat on herself, and for a minute we sat on the berth, side by side, waiting for something to happen.

I remembered Mama's rings,—the diamond and the emerald,—took them off and put them in the toe of my bed-slipper. Then Miss MacFadden whispered, 'They are in Mathilde's room and she is crying.' We then shrieked to Mathilde to give them everything she had and not to try to save anything; but the poor child couldn't hear, and in a second they were at our door, smashing and breaking the window into the corridor. Miss MacFadden said, 'Shall I open the door?' and I said, 'Yes.' In a minute the room was filled with a wild crowd, slashing, threatening, and snatching. One man had cut his hand quite badly. He looked at it stupidly for a minute and then went on pawing things over with the blood streaming. They cut and ripped the bags open with long knives, growling like tigers. When they emptied Miss MacFadden's handbag, I saw one take the red case with my letters of credit and Japanese money, and I tore it out of his hand. Another took her precious string of jade and I managed to get it away from him, only to have it snatched in a minute by another. He bent my fingers back, and in wrenching it out of my hand, broke the string, and the the beads went all over the floor. I was furious and sternly told him to pick them up. Before he realized what he was doing, he did pick up a few of them, then straightened and held a revolver at my head, while I groped for as many as I could find, myself. Miss MacFadden said she thought he was going to blow my brains out, he looked so threatening.

When they had turned everything upside down and inside out, they stood looking at the ruin to see if there was anything more to take. Miss MacFadden thrust into their hands a box of candy they had overlooked and told them it was to eat, and we half pushed them out of the compartment. We thought it was all over and Mathilde joined us, but another party of bandits came rushing in, and in spite of our protests, forced us out of the car, pistols at our backs. One had me by the wrist and pulled me down a steep embankment at a terrific rate of speed. I do not see how I kept my feet. Although there was a moon, the light was too dim to see much, but I could feel long grass around my ankles, and knew that we were going out into the country. We kept together for a time. Poor Miss MacFadden had on mules, and slipped and stumbled so that I actually had to hold her up and keep my eyes on the ground to try and guide her into the smoothest places, but in spite of that she couldn't walk.

190 Outrage at Lincheng

I had planned—as soon as I had a chance—to take my rings out of my slipper, which was terribly thin, and string them on the elastic that held my wrapper around my waist. But I decided I loved Miss MacFadden more than my rings, and after she had tried walking in her bare feet and found it impossible, I tore off the elastic and tied her slippers on. Even then she couldn't keep up, and the bandits kept bringing up ponies for us to ride. We always refused as we didn't want to be separated, and we feared one pony could not hold both of us. Finally I told Miss MacFadden we might as well do it sooner as later, so she was put on a donkey and they managed with great difficulty to get me on the back of a small frisky pony who plunged and kicked. When we first left the train I saw no foreigners and was afraid we were the only people taken. We passed groups of bandits sitting on the ground, sorting and dividing their loot, and at last to my great relief, we came to some of the American men. They seemed to be taking the whole matter as a joke, and a big man was putting on a woman's green hat. Mathilde had been getting on wonderfully: she walked so well that it seemed to me she fairly pranced. I discovered afterward that she had on everything but the kitchen stove: her shoes and stockings, her own dress, and mine—that a bandit had flung at her head in the train—over hers, then on top of that my pale-blue velvet wrapper trimmed with gray fur. She looked like the Queen of Sheba, and was so conspicuous in the dawning light, and so attracted the attention of the bandits, that I made her take it off.

I couldn't notice much after I got on the pony—it was too hard work sticking on. I fortunately had stirrups of a sort tied with string to a makeshift saddle of blankets, and when my feet slipped out, as they sometimes did, I made the bandit who had me in charge put them back, notwithstanding I nearly slid over the pony's head when he went down hill and almost slipped over his tail when he went up hill, until I got the hang of it. On we went, mile after mile, the crowd of bandits around me shifting and changing. They made me think of a pack of wild dogs trotting back and forth, sniffing, growling, and snatching. I cursed the day that the love of color moved me to buy bright jade-green slippers. One old geezer eyed them longingly, but I scowled at him so fiercely that he satisfied himself with tweaking off the pink silk tassel on one side of my wrapper and then trotting around to the other side and pulling off the other. I bossed my bandit terribly. I made him lead my pony most of the time and scolded him when we went too fast. I finally got him so licked into shape that when we went down the steep places, he tried to find the smoothest way, and when we went over stone walls, he pulled the stones down so the pony wouldn't stumble.

It was suddenly light. I passed Mathilde on a donkey with the little Pinger boy in front of her, and shouted at her that I was glad she had him. For a long time a Chinese girl rode stolidly in front of me. I never saw her face, as she never turned. Then I was behind the Mexican bride. I only noticed she had on woollen stockings, below her knees. We were all astride, with no saddles and hardly any clothes. I came to Miss MacFadden standing by her donkey, her glasses gone and a dazed expression on her face. She had been thrown off and they were trying to put her back. I wanted to get off and help her, but they slapped my steed into a trot and I soon left her behind. From that time on I was alone with the bandits.

Our way lay through a valley of cultivated fields of rice and maize, a most peaceful place. I could see miles in front of me a stream of bandits winding over the fields and far away,—thousands of them,—they were not scattered but marched together, apparently four or five abreast. It looked Biblical. I thought of Moses leading the Israelites to the land of Canaan. We were never frightened for a minute, and I never once saw any foreigner who appeared to be. I kept saying over and over to myself, 'We are really captured by bandits and in great danger,' but I couldn't make it seem true. I have a vague impression of passing many people—a Chinese boy of about sixteen supported by two bandits,

192 Outrage at Lincheng

apparently frightened to death; a white man looking at his bare feet, one of which seemed to be paralyzed; a Chinese gentleman holding his silk coat up around his waist like a petticoat (I was surprised to see the beautiful silk in his trousers didn't go way up, for the seat was cotton); bandits of all kinds: one type short, pale yellow, intelligent, another very tall, almost coal-black straggling hair around wild faces and thick cues flapping around their knees,— the last more like animals than human beings,— and I can't say I fancied them, but told them to 'go away' every time they came near me.

We hurried on and on, and just at sunrise came to a little sleeping mud-village. A big gaunt Chinese, the only person visible, watched the procession of half-dressed foreigners as though it were an everyday affair for him. The bandits ran into an onion patch, pulling up the onions and thrusting them in the breasts of their jackets. I shall never smell onions again without thinking of bandits. They all reeked of them. A strange atmosphere for an Oriental outrage! Not at all according to fiction! Some one in the village must have been awake, for I noticed, as we left it behind, that the bandits had kettles of hot water and dishes of hot beansoup. They ate as they hurried on, leaving the dishes carefully by the road to be picked up by the villagers afterward, I suppose.

The bandit who led my pony, when I could persuade him to,—he preferred to drop behind and smoke,—must have been a collector, for he had found a huge white vase (imitation *blanc de Chine*) and carried it tenderly for miles. He probably will sell it later to some guileless American as a bit of Sung porcelain that he 'picked up' in Shantung.

We soon turned to go into the hills, really low mountains that rose on either side of the valley. My poor pony, who had lost his first fine careless rapture after carrying nearly one hundred and seventy pounds for miles, slipped and stumbled over the boulders. His poor little legs trembled and so did mine when they helped me off and I tried to stand after the long rough ride. The bandits wanted me to get on my pony again, but the poor little fellow was really done and I preferred to climb on my own. We started off, a bandit tugging at my wrist, which was soon black and blue, to help me up the steep wall of shifting rock and stone that rose in front of us. Some of the time it was like trying to climb in a coal bin, there were so many loose stones. My heart beat suffocatingly. I told my captor that it was weak and that I'd probably die if I went on at that rate of speed,—a very bad thing for him if I did,—and held his dirty paw over it to show him. He was really very nice and explained to the others, by clapping his hands together very fast, how my heart was acting. He told me by signs that it was because we were so high and afterward let me rest as often as he could.

The first time I sat down, the sun was quite high and I felt it on my bare head. One of the men near me was looking over the things he had stolen and I asked him to let me take a beautiful orange-chiffon scarf he was unfolding to put over by head. To my surprise he gave it to me without a word. I saw a villainous looking Chinese with Miss MacFadden's blue georgette hat on his head, the feather waving in the breeze like the plume on the helmet of Navarre. I had spent hours over that hat, sitting on a hard chair in the little French milliner's, trying to decide if it was becoming, whether it was too heavy for her, and if the feather was the latest thing, and it was too killing to see it on the head of that dirty wretch. He also sported two strings of blue beads that were Mathilde's, and three wristwatches.

Bandits were passing us all the time loaded with loot, and they often stopped me to ask the use of things. One of them had a tube of cold-cream and wanted to know if it was to eat; but I rubbed my cheeks to show him it was a skin food only, and he threw it away. They were terribly interested in the medicine they had stolen and I was consulted about Mothersill's Seasick Remedy, phenacetine, and all kinds of drugs more or less dangerous if taken by the bottleful. I was dying to tell them it was candy, and reduce their number by a few; but a New England conscience is impossible to live down, even in a moment of danger, and I shook my head. Lots of them wore the foreigners' felt hats, held on by winding their cues over the hats and under their chins. They loved the clocks and carried them with a swagger, swinging them from their hands like dinner-pails. I had bought lots of cross-stitch in Shanghai, and one of the bandits wore a folded tray-cloth adorned with peacocks on his head, to keep the sun off. They threw away lots of things I should think they would have found useful—underclothes and so forth—but clung to blankets and sheets. I saw a boy drinking out of my silver powder-box and carefully putting the cover on afterward.

    I was never allowed to rest long at a time, but was dragged on up the hill. When we walked along a steep path above a sheer drop to the valley below, I longed to push my bandit off, for just a touch would have sent him hurtling down to sure death. His grasp on my wrist and the fact that I would probably have gone too were the only things that saved him. When we were nearly to the top, I refused to go any farther, and I sat down surrounded by ten or fifteen, they as glad as I to stop. We were right by a trace of a path and the bandits passed back and forth. Some of them had most interesting chains to fasten their tobacco pouches, very beautiful old carved nuts, and so on. One man had a lovely piece of old white jade with a carved flying-fox as a netsuke. If they had left me any money, I should have tried to buy it. I persuaded several to let me look at their things closely and they were as pleased as Punch when I admired them.

    The view was magnificent, more like the Dolomites than anything I had seen. I couldn't enjoy it long. It had grown warm and one of the bandits sitting just a few feet in front of me took off most of his clothes and began killing cooties. It was an awful sight and I wondered how far a cootie could jump. We were miles up in the air and some of the village boys toiled up to us bringing small teakettles of water. I was awfully thirsty, but there wasn't nearly enough to go around and they wouldn't give me any. They did share their food, such as it was, and gave me thin flat cakes of what looked and tasted like wrapping-paper. They offered me onions and when I refused them, one man gave me a pinch of what looked like tobacco to flavor the tasteless cakes. Papa always said I would eat anything I hadn't seen before, so true to form, I tried this and found it good though the hand that offered it was pretty dirty.

Everybody took a nap after tiffin, so I stretched myself out, my head on a rock—after rubbing my slippers with dirt to make them a little less green—and peacefully went to sleep. Suddenly, someone shook me and pointed to the valley, and down we went again. It was really worse than climbing up. My man dragged me along and we slipped and slid down over the rocks. My chiffon scarf kept slipping over my face like a veil, and every time it did, the bandit put it back for me. I was very conscious of the rings in my slipper, they hurt me every step I took, but I wouldn't think of the pain, I was so determined they shouldn't get them. I thought it was such a good joke that I was walking on the most valuable thing I had and they didn't know it.

We rested for a minute under a small tree just above the village and finally went down to it. It was very quiet and peaceful. Two old men were talking together under a tree in front of the gates and a woman was grinding corn in a primitive hollowed stone. She never even turned to look at me. The sun was very hot. The people brought me a little stool and I sat in the shadow of the gate with my back against the mud wall. Opposite me sat one of the headmen of the village smoking, while a few women and children gathered to look at the 'foreign devil.' I made them understand that I wanted something to drink and that I wanted it hot, so they sent someone to heat water. While we waited I felt a little soft touch on my arm and, turning, saw a little girl scuttling off to hide behind her mother. I tried to get her to talk to me. She wouldn't come but her small brother easily made friends. The man in the gate was very much pleased, as the children were his. I held up my five fingers and told him I had five nephews, showing the different heights. I saw he understood I had five sons and thought it was a great joke. I must have looked pretty wild, as the grandmother of the village brought out the village comb and wanted me to comb my hair. I wish you could have seen it. It was made of wood and looked more like a zoo than a comb. I'm sure if she had put it down, it would have run back to its place on the shelf. I politely declined, the only thing I refused to take from the Chinese women; they were so kind and gentle that I hated to hurt their feelings. When the pot of hot water arrived, I gulped it down though the rice bowl that held it had evidently been used for bean soup. They washed it out before handing it to me, but the rim was still beany and sticky.

I saw a small boy of ten with a little silver fan of mine and borrowed it to keep the sun out of my eyes. He was very proud of it and quite courtly about letting me take it. He was a bright little chap and understood English very well. After he appeared on the scene, he acted as my interpreter for the few minutes longer I staid in the village. Lots of the bandits understood and spoke English, when they wanted to.

Suddenly they pulled me to my feet and motioned that I must go on again. I was frightfully tired and they brought out a chair and tied poles to it to carry me; but the poles were too short and it was too difficult climbing up and over the stones, so they soon abandoned it, and dragged me on. The reason for our haste was the fact that the soldiers were coming up back of us, near enough for the shots to sound loud even to my deaf ears, and looking back once,—I didn't turn again,—they seemed only a few yards away.

We went up a different hill this time, not quite so steep but steep enough, running and stumbling on. Every time the soldiers fell back a little I'd drop to the ground, turn my back, and go to sleep. I thought if I were going to be shot, nothing I could do would keep it from happening, and it would be much nicer to die in my sleep. When the soldiers got too near for comfort, they would wake me up and drag me on. Occasionally one of the wild type of bandit, like a black leopard without the '*bien soigné*' look a leopard has, would run up behind me and push me on violently for a few yards, with his gun at my back. But they would soon tire and leave me to the old man who had led my pony. He was really kind though he growled like a tiger and threatened me with his pistol when I didn't go fast enough to suit him. I knew it was all bluff and it didn't impress me in the least. I scolded him once or twice and told him to stop, but that didn't seem to impress *him*.

We finally reached the top of the hill, quite flat, covered with sparse grass and a few scattered rocks and stones. We all sank down, completely tired out. There were several stone huts and some of the bandits crawled into them—refuges for sheep, I think. Though they were so small that only their bodies were sheltered, they were an escape from the sun and I wished they had offered me one. I pillowed my head on a stone, drew my cape over my head and went to sleep again. I was perfectly convinced that we were in for a week or two at the shortest and wanted to save my strength. It was so high the wind blew cold, and I asked a bandit to give me the white counterpane he was sitting on—part of his loot. He gave it up very reluctantly and never left my side until he got it back. It was an old-fashioned honey-comb spread, like the ones I used to see at my grandmother's when I was a child. I wonder where it came from.

I couldn't sleep long; my Chinese friends kept shaking me unceremoniously to ask me questions. Though we were miles from the village, one man I had never seen before woke me up, held up his hand with five fingers spread and pointed at me with questioning pride. I started to explain that I had five nephews, not sons; but remembering the Chinese reverence for the mother of many sons, decided to adopt the boys thrust upon me and lose my reputation as well as everything else I had brought with me to Shantung. Doctor Houghton told me afterward that probably the tale of the size of my family had gone all over the country.

I had no sooner dozed off again than another bandit poked me, handed me a man's clean collar and a pencil, and made me understand by signs that he wanted me to write the word for collar. I did, then pointing at his gun I wrote G U N. In a minute I was surrounded by an admiring crowd, like children all wanting to see. One had a beautiful new red-rubber hot-water bottle. After I had written HOT-WATER BOTTLE on the collar, they tried to have me explain what it was used for. The owner pretended to drink out of it, but I shook my head. Then he held it to his mouth and blew to ask if it were a cushion. Again I shook my head and said 'hot water,' which they seemed to understand. I then held it first to my stomach and then to my ear, with groans and grimaces of imaginary pain, and they finally got it through their heads, to our mutual delight, what the thing was for. The owner loved it and was terribly afraid someone would take it away from him.

As they squatted around me in a circle, all of us laughing, an awfully nice-looking young man joined us. He was neatly dressed, about twenty-five or thirty, I should think,—though it is difficult to tell the age of a Chinese,—and evidently a person of authority. The other men were more or less stolid, some of them badly frightened when the soldiers came too near, but he seemed to have a real flair for adventure and was having the time of his life. He pointed proudly to the soldiers' hats and jackets he and one or two of the others wore, and held an imaginary gun to his shoulder. I couldn't quite make out whether he was trying to tell me they had been soldiers or that they had captured the uniforms from soldiers they had just killed. I told him I was cold. He understood English perfectly and took off his own coat and threw it around me and buttoned it under my chin himself. That left him so unprotected in the sharp wind that I didn't want to take it, and told him he would freeze, and urged him to take it back. He finally did and sent one of his men for an English coat, evidently taken from one of the men on the train. I couldn't put it on over my cape and when I stood in the wind in only my nightgown and little pink-satin wrapper, I felt so unprotected in front of my Chinese audience that

I got the Bandit Chief—I'm sure he was that—to hold my cape like a screen while I put the coat on underneath. We sat down in the circle again. He took his little case out of his pocket and showed me his toothbrush and a piece of silver: fifty cents—all the money he had. He then sent for a rice bowl of bean soup, hot and good, though rather tasteless. All the bandits were constantly urging me to eat, but I was so thirsty I couldn't swallow and they hadn't enough water themselves to spare any for me. They offered me cigarettes too, and when I tried to make them understand that I didn't smoke, they thought it was the cigarettes I didn't like, so the Chief sent for a cigar, which I really hated not to take, he was so anxious to give me something.

Suddenly the bandit next to me jabbed his revolver against my heart. I laughed and told him he couldn't frighten me that way. In a few minutes, with a frightful scowl he did it again. I laughed again. It really did amuse me, as I didn't think for a minute he would shoot me down in cold blood. The Chief patted me on the back the second time and held up his thumb above his closed fist. I will confess I was terribly pleased and flattered to have a bandit call me Number One. The chief bandit drew his revolver out of his belt and handed it to me, watching me with amused eyes. I handled it up and down and said, 'very heavy' and gave it back. He gave it to me again; this time I shuddered and pushed it away. He showed me a jade ring that he wore, the stone turned into the palm of his hand. Although he was treating me almost like an honored guest, he wasn't above pointing at me and then at the ring with an insinuating smile, to ask me if I had any. I shook my head sadly, waving my hand in the direction of the holdup, murmured 'All gone' dramatically, and drew my feet tighter under my cape.

When he told me my slippers were too thin to walk in and tried to make me put on a new pair of Chinese shoes he sent for, I began to think he was getting too 'warm,' as they say in Hide the Thimble, and I looked about to see where I could put my rings. I said that Chinese feet were smaller than mine and he didn't insist, but I was afraid that the subject might come up again, and then too, my slippers were wearing through. Just beside me was a low rock split down the middle, the crack about two inches wide and four or five deep. It was an ideal hiding-place, as across the crack was a thin diamond-shaped stone that I thought would serve to mark the spot. Very quietly I drew my cape over my feet and over the stone, took off my slipper and buried the rings. I had to be very careful, as I was surrounded by Chinese, and I was relieved when it was safely done. I then stuck my feet out in front of me and innocently said, 'They are getting cold.' I didn't quite dare to suggest the Chinese shoes, but I accepted a pair of men's socks they gave me and promptly put them on. It was just about five o'clock, because one of the bandits who was wearing a wrist watch—probably looted—showed me the time. My nice bandit chief started to leave me. I felt so safe with him that I wanted him to take me with him but he smilingly shook his head. Half way down the hill he turned, and gayly waved his hand to me in parting, and I never saw him again. Before he went I told him he was much too good and bright for such work, and when I added, 'Do you understand?' he gravely bowed his head in assent. I told him he should come to America and start over again, but the thought of how impossible that was made me dumb.

After I had finished writing words for the amusement of the bandits I wrote a note on the collar to Mr. Atkinson of the Standard Oil Company, telling him where I was, as far as I knew. I held it out to the men saying, 'Mei foo, mei foo,' the Chinese for Standard Oil in Shanghai, but they either didn't understand or pretended not to, and threw it on the ground. It was still there when they pulled me to my feet to start on again, and I had a vague hope that someone might find it and send it on.

This time the middle-aged man who dragged me off the train disappeared, and his place was taken by a younger, stronger Chinese. The soldiers must have been very near as we started down the hill at top speed. It was very steep and as I climbed down from rock to rock I felt like the human fly. The men acted frightened and the mob spirit is very contagious and I found myself hurrying, hurrying just as they did; in spite of this I couldn't go as fast as they wanted me to, and my bandit insisted, in spite of my protests, on taking me on his back, not realizing how heavy I was, but he soon flattened and had to crawl out from under me. Then he dragged me on as fast as he could by my wrist. Just in front of me were two bandits, half supporting, half carrying a Chinese gentleman. He sank to the ground and the wilder of his captors began to beat him with the stick he carried. He tried to struggle to his feet and I saw his face gleam white, impassive, for a moment, and then he fell again. The men went wild and fired at his prostrate body until he no longer moved. The one who had beaten him joined my bandit in pulling me along. I soon wished him away, as he was still crazy with excitement and very rough.

When we got to the valley, they put me on a poor little donkey whose back was already piled high with a thick pack of looted coats and blankets, with no saddle, no stirrups, and no bridle. Of course I slipped and slid. They tried to hold me on, but the rough brute grabbed my arm so hard he pulled me off instead of holding me on. I was so angry that I scolded him and he began to beat me; but my coat and cape were so thick I didn't feel it—it only made me more angry.

In back of us were the soldiers and in front of us a terrific storm was coming up—copper-colored clouds slashed with lightning. They were frightened and soon pulled me off the donkey and started running, dragging me between them and pointing to the clouds. I think I must have run a mile, panting and stumbling, before I became so exhausted even the bandits saw I could go no farther. I was streaming with perspiration and took off my cape, giving it to the kind bandit, and so thirsty that my lips were covered with a dry cottonlike substance. At last my bandit said, in perfectly good English, 'My wife lives in that village; you go there,' and gave me a little push toward a small town I hadn't noticed before in the dusk. I turned obediently and trotted down between the paddy fields thinking my two companions were of course following. In a second I found I was alone, the others having rushed on. The rain was already beginning to come down in big drops and by the time I got to the gates of the town the storm had commenced. I found myself standing or trying to stand in front of closed wooden gates set in a blank mud-wall. The gates were on a chain, and peeking in the crack I could see a donkey and nothing beyond but blackness. The rain was coming down in sheets, turning the dust into a sea of liquid mud in which I slipped and slid in my thin slippers. I pounded and pounded with my hands on the closed gates, crying. 'Let me in, let me in,' but no one answered. I was soon wet to the waist and so tired that I sat down in the mud as near the gate as I could get, drawing my knees up and trying to find an inch of shelter. When it began to hail I looked about to find some place I could crawl into, as I saw there was no use trying to get into the village, though I felt sure they had heard me. There were no buildings, nothing but the blank wall; but just in front of the gate was a tiny tent-like hut thatched with straw and with straw in the bottom. I could just manage to get in on my hands and knees; it was too small to sit up in, but I curled up on my side and drew my feet in as far as I could. It was very hard to change my position, but I did it as often as possible, as I was sure I was in a dog-house and didn't want to get too stiff to kick an inhospitable dog when he came home in the morning.

The rain blew in on me; in spite of my shivers I managed to sleep a great part of the night, and when I was awake I couldn't help chuckling to think that here was I, who am never allowed by my family to sleep without some one in the room next to me with the door open,—because of my deafness,—alone in a hostile China, sleeping on the ground and 'getting away with it.' Once I got so cold I backed out to have one more try at the gate. While I was pounding and shouting, I saw about a hundred yards away a group of men running and struggling. When they began shooting I realized that every time it lightened I was silhouetted against the gate, and I was afraid they would take a shot at me or else recapture me, so I ran back to my dog-house, to stay until morning, this time. I was really quite uncomfortable; my head jammed against the thatch so that it made my neck stiff and when I managed to turn, my hair caught and pulled. I was still frightfully thirsty and tried to force my hand through the straw and get some of the hail, big as marbles, just out of my reach. I woke up at dawn with a jerk as though I had been called, and still haunted by the idea of the dog, scrambled out as best I could. No one was in sight as I walked feebly up to the still closed gates. I looked through the crack before I started to pound, and found myself gazing into the eyes of at least fifty Chinese men. I have no idea how long they had been standing there immovable, silent, waiting for the strange something that had been battering at their gates in the night to materialize. The sight of me didn't seem to reassure them, and I was the first to break the menacing silence. I begged them to let me in, trying to put a sob into my voice though I was really very much on guard, watching their expression and trying to guess their attitude. They were afraid of me, I think, and wouldn't open the gates for several minutes, and then not before they had searched me to see if I carried any concealed weapons. When I finally did get in, one old lady took possession of me and led me across a little courtyard to a mud seat in the opening leading to the mud houses beyond. The men lost their interest and disappeared, going out to their work in the fields, but I was instantly surrounded, altogether too near for comfort, by a crowd of women and children. The young boys, ragged and dirty, fought each other for places in the front line. Almost all were deeply pitted with smallpox, and I imagined that the few who weren't were coming down with it. My old lady was wonderfully bright or else knew a little English. She seemed to understand everything I said and told the others what to do. She smoothed my hair gently back from my face, tried to pick the straw out of it, and sat down beside me holding my hand. All the women were terribly curious. They couldn't understand why I was so white,—they were all very black,—and pawed my face, looked closely at the palms of my hands, pulled my wrapper down to pat my neck and lifted it up to look at my ankles. They were evidently anxious to see if I was white all over. I could stand that, but when they began to poke their hands in my mouth to touch the gold band on one tooth, I thought that was too much and laughingly pushed them away. They asked me in pantomime where I had slept. I pointed to the ground and they looked at each other with sympathy. A younger woman brought me food, bean broth in a rice-bowl and a Chinese biscuit of white flour to break into it, but I was so thirsty I couldn't eat, and eagerly waited for the water they had made me understand they were heating for me. It was finally brought to me by an old hag (probably about my own age!) covered with rags, and so dirty. She knelt and sucked the spout of the teapot with her withered lips before she poured the water into a bowl for me. I couldn't refuse to drink it—I was dying of thirst—but I had visions of coming down with all sorts of Oriental diseases if I ever got out.

All of the women I saw had tiny bound feet. Though there was no visible water to wash with and almost none to drink, most of them were comparatively neat. They had a look of being sewed into their clothes, and I wondered how long they had had them on—probably all winter. One young woman, much better dressed than the others, came for a minute to look at me from the edge of the crowd. After gazing at me curiously as though I were a captured mermaid or something equally strange, she turned away without a word. When I told Doctor Houghton about her, he said she must have been shy, but I have an idea she was a social leader and, as the children say, 'stuck-up.'

While I waited for the hot water, an ancient man appeared, clothed in a long silk garment. I have an impression too of a hat and a venerable straggling beard, like John's porcelains. With a bow he handed me a scroll-like paper on which was a line of beautifully written Chinese characters. He gave me a block of ink and a brush and waited. I didn't know exactly what was expected of me but wrote or rather painted my name and address and with an equally low bow, handed it back. He too disappeared and I never saw him again. (It may have been the head man of the village, and this a report to the local magistrate in case of trouble.)

I had a little lace on my wrapper and all the Chinese, even the bandits, loved it and fingered it longingly. I tore off a piece with a ribbon rose, gave it to the young woman who fed me, and she carefully carried it away. They really seemed crazy about lace, and Mathilde told me afterward that she saw a young bandit wearing a real-lace brassière of mine.

I never saw such hair as I saw on one man who was combing out his pigtail. In spite of his head being shaven back to his ears, his hair—thick as a horse's tail—came below his knees.

I soon got tired of sitting up straight on a hard mud seat and being pulled and pawed, even if they were friendly. The sun was beginning to get hot too, and I had lost my scarf the night before in my wild trot to the village. My young friend stood in front of me to keep the sun off, but I couldn't keep my head up any longer, and persuaded her to take me into her house to rest, which she did at last, very reluctantly. It was just a dark mud-room. The only thing I could see was the kang covered with blue covers and a lone hen in a box. It was such a blessed relief to lie down, using my coat as a pillow and protect my hair. I didn't even mind when the Chinese woman tucked me up with her own covers, though I remembered the tales I had been told of the vermin in the villages of the interior. I wasn't troubled at all then or ever, though I suppose I should have ultimately been a victim if I had stayed in captivity long. All the village came in squads to look at me and I found it easier if I kept my eyes closed. If they thought me asleep, the women didn't try to talk to me, and I think I really did sleep a good deal. Once I woke up to find the room crowded with men, all gazing silently and respectfully. I made the woman among them understand I couldn't breathe and she shooed them out.

The Chinese in the interior are terribly curious about foreigners. Mr. Holden told me that when he went on business trips, they crowded about him so that he had almost to throw them out before he had room to eat. My heart bled for those kind women, I can't imagine people existing with so little. They have clothes to cover them, and walls, a little food (this is a famine district), almost no water. One of the nurses at the Peking Union Medical College told me of an old lady of seventy who was given her first bath at the hospital. She was frightened to death when she saw the water and didn't know what they were going to do to her, but later grew to love it. I wish I could go back to carry them—not religion, or even food, but a little beauty, bright colors, pictures, something to look at. It seems absurd, but they did love my pink crêpe-de-chine nightgown so, even if it was torn and stained with mud, and stroked the embroidery with admiration.

I must have dozed a good deal, because it was afternoon when a Chinese in uniform of a sort came into the hut with the young woman and made me get up and go with him. I was very comfortable and the villagers were so kind that I hated to, and hung back, but they all seemed anxious to have me leave. I realize now that they knew he was taking me out, but I thought I recognized him as the bandit who had sent me to the village the night before and was sure he had come back to get me and take me further into the mountains. Suddenly an overwhelming feeling of curiosity, a desire to 'go, look, see,' and perhaps a little spirit of adventure made me want to go on and find out what was around the next corner, figuratively speaking, and I went without a word. The woman tied a little square of blue linen over my head and bade me good-bye. My bandit soldier knelt in the dust while I mounted from his knee to the back of another small donkey, and we started on. I never looked back but, keeping my eyes on the sun-drenched landscape in front of me, wondered where we were going. It was all very commonplace, no sign of the storm or the bandits of the night before, just fields and an occasional man cultivating them.

I was riding bareback this time with only a blanket. I tried to cling to the poor little beast with my knees in the approved fashion, but I was so tired my legs shook and I couldn't get a good grip. The bandit seemed to be in a great hurry, and as we didn't go fast enough to suit him he beckoned to a youth in a rice field to come and lead the donkey while he held me on and beat the beast at the same time. We went very fast then and must have been a weird sight, galloping between the paddy fields. After many miles we came to another village. Over the closed gates stood a group of men, ten or perhaps fifteen, all with stern, threatening faces, aiming guns at our heads. We rode straight up under them without a pause and I sat quietly waiting while my escort argued with them. He must have convinced them that we were harmless, as they came down at last and opened the gates. They didn't like me well enough to ask me in, but a fine-looking, well-dressed Chinese came out and gave me and my guide tea in cups. He poured cup after cup from the teapot he carried and I couldn't get enough.

I had slipped off my donkey to rest a minute, but soon had to mount again and ride on. The sun was very hot, and when we stopped at another town and I rode into an almost fortified courtyard apart from the rest of the village, I hoped from the bottom of my heart that we had at last arrived wherever we were going; but I found that it was only to leave the donkey, who was all in, and no wonder, poor dear. How to carry me on was a problem. At first, after much searching for rope, they brought out a chair, quite an interesting old carved one, to rig up as a palanquin. As before, the poles were too short and this time the men who carried me too old to go far, and just outside the walls they put me down in despair. Then they hunted up a Shanghai wheelbarrow. My blue handkerchief wouldn't stay tied under my chin, and while they were making a cushion of hay for me to sit on I asked an old woman for a pin. Of course she didn't have one, but from somewhere in her ragged garments she brought out a needle with a bit of thread—evidently a great treasure—and sewed my handkerchief on in back and under my chin, making a sort of cap.

We started off, the bandit on one side of the wheelbarrow and I on the other, so near that I felt as though I had my arms around his neck. The old man who wheeled us staggered and lurched and the bandit commandeered three boys working in a near-by field, and with the three harnessed abreast to pull us in front, and the old man to steady us behind, we bumped over the stones so fast that I felt as though my teeth and eyes would drop out of my head. I tried to make them go slower but they only laughed and went faster. My bandit took out his purse and showed me a piece of money. I think he may have been asking for a reward, but I ignored it and he put it back without pressing the matter. This was the only time anyone even hinted at ransom.

I had been able for some time to see in the distance the smoking chimneys of what seemed to be a large town, but I never for an instant suspected I was being rescued. I suppose fatigue made me stupid. At any rate, I was overcome with surprise when my coach and four drew up at a little railroad station and I was surrounded in an instant by a crowd of excited soldiers and railway men. Mr. Nailla, [sic] a good-looking young American of the Asia Development Company, rushed out and helped me to the station. I asked Mr. Nailla the minute I saw him, 'How much did you have to pay to get me out?' and was delighted when he said, 'Not one cent.' He told me he had been walking around all day with $50,000 in his pocket, but it hadn't been needed as yet. To my very great relief he told me that Miss MacFadden and Mathilde had gotten out that morning and were safe in the hospital at Tsinan-fu. I hadn't worried about them much. I didn't see any reason why the Chinese shouldn't treat them just as well as they did me, but it was pleasant to hear just the same.

Mr. Nailla was a ideal rescuer—handsome, cheerful, executive, and having the time of his life. He looked absolutely worn out, as he had had no sleep for two days and a night, but I can't say that he acted tired. He thought of everything at once for my comfort, gave me a pocket handkerchief, sent for tea and eggs, and then said, 'Now, Miss Aldrich, I am going to get you a pair of Chinese trousers.' This was a terrible shock and I thought for the first time of how I must look. My face was streaked with dirt, the skin peeling off my nose from sunburn, and my hair, tangled with straw, was hanging down my back. I had on a man's coat buttoned to my chin and reaching to my knees. Below that my wrapper and nightgown hung in shreds, caked with mud. Mr. Nailla said, 'Miss MacFadden's feet were in a frightful condition. How are yours?' I told him, 'All right,' but he insisted upon taking off my slippers, and found my feet blistered and torn by my rings. I had been so excited I hadn't felt it. The wife and daughter of the stationmaster took me to their room, bathed my face and feet, and fitted me out with new trousers and stockings. They were too kind for words and wouldn't take a cent in return. We were off the main line and we started the journey back to such civilization as there is in China, at present, in a baggage car, I lying in a wicker steamer-chair supplied by the station woman. Though I wanted to sit up, lying down seemed to be expected of me. Mr. Nailla perched in front of the open sliding door, swinging his feet. I felt as though we were all under fire and was terribly afraid I would be hit by a stray bullet.

I was introduced to the Chinese officers of the rescuing party, but when they began to question me as to the whereabouts of the bandits Mr. Nailla put his finger on his lips and I 'went to sleep' again. When we reached the Express we were met by the Catholic Mission Father. He was a big man with a beard and beamed with sympathy and kindness. He and Mr. M—— and another Asia Development man, wanted to carry me from one train to the other. I was perfectly able to walk and wouldn't hear of it. It was the same train that had been held up and I had a whole car to myself.

The train boy made up a bed in one of the compartments, but first brought me a most elaborate dinner from soup to dessert. While I was stuffing, my bandit appeared at the door, gazed at the food almost in tears, and nibbled at his fingers to show me he wanted to be fed too. I was too astonished to more than stare at him and Mr. M—— coming back just then, the man vanished. I said, 'My bandit was just here begging for food.' Mr. M—— looked at me as though he thought I needed a little ice on my head and said, 'Oh, Miss Aldrich, he couldn't have been. All Chinese look alike. It must have been one of the soldiers.' I didn't insist, as I was afraid he might think I was delirious, but when he went to hunt some woman on the train who would be willing to lend me hairpins the bandit appeared at once, like the Cheshire cat's smile. This time I filled his hands with bread before he vanished. Back came Mr. M—— very much amused. 'By Jove, it is your bandit; what shall we do with him?' I said, 'Feed him up,' and trailed out into the car to see that it was done. They gave him money enough to buy food and took him away. For the rest of the time I amused myself drawing a map of the place where I had hidden my rings to send back to Mr. Nailla. He had promised to find them for me if I could tell him where they were.

We reached Tsinan-fu about eleven in the evening and I found Mrs. Nailla, the American Consul, and Mr. Babcock, the Standard Oil man, waiting for me on the platform. Mr. Babcock already had the bandit in charge, and almost the first thing I heard was 'Miss Aldrich, what do you want done with your bandit?' — a question I was to hear repeated many times before I left China. Mr. Babcock offered to take him home, but I was afraid he might have a relapse and it was arranged to keep him at the station. The poor thing looked so forlorn, I patted him on the back and told him that they would take good care of him. He probably understood nothing but the pat, but that seemed to cheer him.

A great many of our experiences were amusing, but I found myself quite shocked when one of my friends in Japan said she wished she had been captured too. It made me realize that I had dwelt only on the amusing side. It is far from funny to lose all one's little treasures as well as the things that are valuable and difficult to replace. It must have been dreadful beyond words for Mrs. Allen and Mrs. Pinger to have their children torn from them in the darkness of a strange country by a wild horde of armed Chinese. If it is terrifying to tourists who can leave at the least hint of danger or who can give up their trip to China entirely because of the disturbed conditions, forgetting in France or England that such a country exists, what must it be to the many American and other foreigners who live there? Their children, their homes, their money—all safe if nothing happens, but swept away in any instant if there is any trouble.

If a man goes even a little way into the interior on a business trip, his wife doesn't know whether she will see him again in a day or two or not. He may be carried off by bandits to spend months unheard from, and there is always the possibility that he may never come back at all. They carry their constant fear very bravely, even gayly, but I am sure it is there. Someone told me the other day that the Chinese Government had announced that they would pay no indemnity for 'shattered nerves.' No wonder—they would be supporting half of the foreign population if they did.

Once when Mrs. H—— and I came back from shopping, we were met by the gate-boy with, 'We can't find Benny.' I saw the color drop out of her cheeks and the terror come into her eyes. My knees shook as we searched the compound. How awful if that boy had been kidnapped! Of course he hadn't been; he had only sat down just outside under a bush to catch insects; but we were both very much frightened for a few minutes before we found him. Mrs. H—— looked ill for days.

The words, 'Lest we forget,' on the walls of the Legation Compound—in memory of the Boxer trouble in 1900—are growing faint, and I am afraid they are fading out of the hearts of many people. I am not clever enough to make any suggestions; but I wish in some way the United Powers could impress China with the fact that if she is ever to be the greatest country she is capable of being, she must mend her ways.

Your loving sister,
Lucy Aldrich.

NOTES

CHAPTER ONE

1. Paul Hutchinson, *China's Real Revolution* (New York: National Council Department of Missions, 1924), 10.

2. Lucy Aldrich, "A Week-End With Chinese Bandits," *Atlantic Monthly* (November 1923), 672.

3. John Powell, "The Bandits' 'Golden Eggs' Depart," *Asia* (December 1923) (hereafter cited as "Golden Eggs").

4. Peking & Tientsin *Times*, 9 May 1923.

5. Aldrich, "A Week-End With Chinese Bandits," 680.

6. Ibid., 684.

7. Ibid., 686.

8. *The China Press* (Shanghai), 8 May 1923.

CHAPTER TWO

1. *The China Press*, 8 May 1923.

2. Milbourne to Hughes, 12 May 1923, Department of State General Records, Record Group 59, 393.1123 Lincheng/142, National Archives, Washington, D. C. (hereafter cited as RG 59, 393.1123).

3. Ibid.

4. Bell to Hughes, 9 May 1923, *Foreign Relations of the U.S.*, Vol. 1 (Washington, D. C. 1938) (hereafter cited as *Foreign Relations*), 633.

5. Milbourne to Hughes, 12 May 1923, RG 59, 393.1123/142.

CHAPTER THREE

1. Derk Bodde, *China's Cultural Tradition* (New York: Holt, Rinehart & Winston, 1965), 7.

2. Ibid., p. 8.

3. E. Estlin Cummings, *E. E. Cummings, Complete Poems* (New York: Harcourt, Brace, Jovanovich, 1972), 515.

4. John K. Fairbank, Edwin O. Reischauer, and Albert M. Craig, *East Asia the Modern Transformation* (Boston: Houghton Mifflin, 1965), 63.

5. Samuel L. Clemens, *Letters From the Earth* (New York: Harper & Row, 1962), 20.

6. Fairbank, *East Asia the Modern Transformation*, 75.

7. Ibid., 76.

8. Richard Stremski, *Britain's China Policy 1920-1928* (Ann Arbor: University Microfilms), 1.

9. Fairbank, *East Asia the Modern Transformation*, 77.

10. Ibid.

11. John K. Fairbank and Ssu-Yu Teng, *China's Response to the West* (New York: Atheneum, 1969), 24.

12. Fairbank, *East Asia the Modern Transformation*, 140.

13. Molly J. Coye and Jon Livingston, *China Yesterday & Today* (New York: Bantam, 1975), 151.

14. Leon Hellerman and Alan L. Stein, *China: Readings on the Middle Kingdom* (New York: Washington Square Press, 1971), 153.

15. Fairbank, *East Asia the Modern Transformation*, 146.

16. Molly J. Coye, *China Yesterday & Today*, 152.

17. Fairbank, *East Asia the Modern Transformation*, 342.

18. Ibid., 167.

19. Richard C. DeAngelis, *Jacob Gould Schurman & American Policy Toward China 1921-1925* (Ann Arbor: University Microfilms), 120.

20. Ibid., 126-7.

21. Ibid., 222.

22. Ibid., 223.

23. Ibid., 224-5.

24. Ibid., 227.

25. Ibid., 228.

26. Ibid., 229-30.

CHAPTER FOUR

1. North China *Herald* (Shanghai), 19 May 1923.

2. Pinger to Huston, 16 June 1923, RG 59, 393.1123.

3. John Powell, *My 25 Years in China* (New York: Macmillan, 1945), 99.

4. Powell, " 'Esteemed Guests' of the Chinese Bandits," *Asia,* November 1923, 857.

5. *New York Times*, 16 May 1923.

6. Schurman to Hughes, 12 May 1923, RG 59, 393.1123/43.

7. Powell, "Esteemed Guests," 858.

8. Powell, *My 25 Years in China,* 104-5.

9. Peking & Tientsin *Times,* 12 May 1923.

CHAPTER FIVE

1. Brown to Macleay, 8 May 1923, Public Record Office, FO 371/9190 X/K6471 (hereafter cited as FO 371 with additional identifying letters and numbers).

2. Schurman to Hughes, 20 June 1923, RG 59, 393.1123/207.

3. Powell, "Golden Eggs," 914-5.

4. *New York Times,* 18 May 1923.

5. North China *Herald.* 7 July 1923.

6. Powell, "Golden Eggs," 914-5.

7. John Gunther, *Inside Asia* (New York: Harper & Row, 1939), 146.

Notes 217

8. Stuart Schram, *Mao-Tse-Tung* (Middlesex, England: Pelican, 1966), 52.

9. Edgar Snow, *Red Star Over China* (New York: Bantam, 1979), 153.

10. Schurman to Hughes, 26 July 1923, RG 59, 393.1123/219.

11. Others: Chou Tien-sung; Chin Kwang-chu; Chao Cheng-lao; Tung Foh-lou; Tou Erh-yu; Yen Chen-shan. See: Chen Wu-wo, *True Facts About the Lincheng Incident* (Peking Express Press, 1923), 8.

12. Chen Wu-wo, *True Facts*, 10.

CHAPTER SIX

1. Reginal Rowlatt, affidavit, RG 59, 393.1123.

2. Powell, *China Weekly Review* (Shanghai), May 1923.

3. *Trans-Pacific,* 9 June 1923.

4. Ibid.

5. *China Weekly Review*, Powell's letter of 17 May 1923.

6. *New York Times*, 19 May 1923.

7. Powell, *China Weekly Review*, May 1923.

8. Powell, "Esteemed Guests," 858.

9. Powell, *My 25 Years in China*, 109.

10. North China *Herald*, 26 May 1923.

11. Powell, "Esteemed Guests," 869.

12. Ibid.

13. North China *Herald*, 26 May 1923.
14. RG 59, 393.1123, news clippings.
15. North China *Herald*, 26 May 1923.

CHAPTER SEVEN

1. Peking & Tientsin *Times*, 11 May 1923.
2. Milbourne to Hughes, 12 May 1923, RG 59, 393.1123/142.
3. Ibid.
4. Ibid.
5. Ibid.
6. Ibid.
7. Ibid.
8. Ibid.
9. DeAngelis, *Schurman*, 231 note 37.
10. Macleay to Curzon, 12 May 1923, FO 371.9190 F1874/22/10.
11. RG 59, 393.1123.
12. Milbourne to Hughes, 12 May 1923, RG 59, 393.1123/142.
13. Macleay to Curzon, 12 May 1923, FO 371/9190 F1874/22/10.
14. Milbourne to Hughes, 12 May 1923, RG 59, 393.1123/142.

15. Bell to Hughes, 16 May 1923, *Foreign Relations*, 639.

16. Bell to Hughes, 14 May 1923, *Foreign Relations*, 637.

17. North China *Herald*, 19 May 1923.

18. Bell to Hughes, 16 May 1923, *Foreign Relations*, 639-40.

19. Schurman to Hughes, 18 May 1923, *Foreign Relations*, 641.

20. DeAngelis, *Schurman*, 233.

21. Schurman to Hughes, 18 May 1923, *Foreign Relations*, 641.

22. Ibid.

23. Schurman to Hughes, 19 May 1923, RG 59, 393.1123/62.

24. Ibid.

25. Macleay to Curzon, 10 June 1923, FO371/9190 F2166/22/10.

26. Schurman to Hughes, 20 May 1923, RG 59, 303.1123/67.

27. Schurman to Hughes, 20 May 1923, *Foreign Relations*, 644.

CHAPTER EIGHT

1. Gunther, *Inside Asia*, 146.

2. Dennis Bloodsworth, *The Chinese Looking Glass* (New York: Farrar, Straus & Giroux, 1966), 169.

3. John Stoddard, *John L. Stoddard's Lectures*, China & Japan (Chicago: Schuman, 1897), 298.

4. Fairbank *East Asia the Modern Transformation*, 21.

5. Bloodsworth, *The Chinese Looking Glass*, 365.

6. Ibid.

7. Bradley Smith and Wan-go Weng, *China, A History In Art* (New York: Doubleday), 235.

8. Smith, *China, A History In Art*, 233.

9. Bloodsworth, *The Chinese Looking Glass*, 35.

10. Coye, *China Yesterday & Today*, 138.

11. Fairbank, *China's Response to the West*, 17.

12. Fairbank, *East Asia the Modern Transformation*, 49.

13. Smith, *China, A History In Art*, 250.

14. Fairbank, *China's Response to the West*, 19.

15. E. Backhouse and J. Bland, *Annals & Memoirs of the Court of Peking* (London: William Heinemann, 1914), 327-331.

16. Bloodsworth, *The Chinese Looking Glass*, 356.

17. Fairbank, *China's Response to the West*, 25.

18. Fairbank, *East Asia the Modern Transformation*, 144.

19. Fairbank, *China's Response to the West*, 30.

20. Ibid., 63.

21. Ibid., 89.

22. Han Suyin, *The Crippled Tree* (Great Britain: Panther, 1965), 85.

23. Fairbank, *China's Response to the West,* 175.

24. Der Ling, *Two Years in the Forbidden City* (New York: Dodd Mead, 1924), 112a.

25. DeAngelis, *Schurman,* 91.

26. Han Suyin, *A Mortal Flower* (Great Britain: Panther, 1966), 46.

27. DeAngelis, *Schurman,* 97.

28. Fairbank, *East Asia the Modern Transformation,* 653.

29. Odoric Wou, *Militarism in Modern China: The Career of Wu Pei-Fu, 1916-1939* (Ann Arbor: University Microfilms), 65.

30. Han Suyin, *A Mortal Flower,* 45.

31. *The Living Age,* "Blue Trains and Bandits" (Autumn 1923), 451-2.

32. Chu Pao-chin, *V. K. Wellington Koo, A Study of the Diplomat and Diplomacy of Warlord China During His Early Career, 1919-1924* (Ann Arbor: University Microfilms), 101. Hereafter cited as *V. K. Wellington Koo.*

33. Han Suyin, *A Mortal Flower,* 146.

34. Han Suyin, *The Crippled Tree,* 115-16.

35. Hutchinson, *China's Real Revolution,* 27-8.

CHAPTER NINE

1. H. G. W. Woodhead, Ed., *The Chian Year Book 1924-1925 (Tientsin:* 1183.

2. Chen Wu-wo, *True Facts,* 6.

3. Ibid., 13.

4. Bell to Hughes, 9 May 1923, *Foreign Relations*, 633.

5. Chen Wu-wo, *True Facts*, 13-14.

6. Ibid., 13.

7. Ibid., 16.

8. Bell to Hughes, 11 May 1923, *Foreign Relations*, 636.

9. Chu Pao-chin, *V. K. Wellington Koo*, 198.

10. *China Review* (June 1923), 263.

11. North China *Herald*, 19 May 1923.

12. Peking & Tientsin *Times*, 19 May 1923.

13. Bell to Hughes, 14 May 1923, *Foreign Relations*, 637.

14. North China *Herald*, 26 May 1923.

15. Peking & Tientsin *Times*, 17 May 1923.

16. Bell to Hughes, 16 May 1923, *Foreign Relations*, 639.

17. Schurman to Hughes, 20 June 1923, RG 59, 393.1123/207.

18. *New York Times*, 17 May 1923 and *China Review*, June 1923, 262.

19. *Trans-Pacific*, 9 June 1923.

20. North China *Herald*, 26 May 1923.

21. RG 59, 393.1123, news clippings.

22. North China *Herald*, 26 May 1923.

23. Ibid.

24. Chen Wu-wo, *True Facts*.

Notes 223

CHAPTER TEN

1. Pinger to Huston, 16 June 1923, RG 59, 393.1123.

2. *New York Times*, 19 May 1923.

3. FO 371/9190 reprint of *Daily Telegraph* of 11 June 1923.

4. Powell, "Esteemed Guests," 859.

5. RG 59, 393.1123, news clippings.

6. Naylor to MacMurry, 21 May 1923, RG 59, 393.1123.

7. Schurman to Hughes, 23 May 1923, *Foreign Relations*, 645.

8. RG 59, 393.1123, news clippings.

9. Powell, "Golden Eggs," 915.

10. Powell, *My 25 Years in China,* 112-113.

11. Chen Wu-wo, *True Facts*, 21.

12. Macleay to Curzon, 10 June 1923, FO 371/9190 F2166/22/10.

13. Schurman to Hughes, 23 May 1923, *Foreign Relations*, 644.

14. North China *Daily News*, 22 May 1923.

15. RG 59, 393.1123, news clippings.

16. Macleay to Curzon, 10 June 1923, FO 371/9190 F2166/22/10

17. Ibid.

18. North China *Herald*, 2 June 1923.

19. Liu Tseu-chin & Chen Hwan-ting, North China *Herald*, 2 June 1923.

20. Chen Wu-wo, *True Facts*, 23.

21. Powell, "Golden Eggs," 916.

22. Peking & Tientsin *Times*, 26 May 1923.

23. Edna Lee Booker, *News Is My Job* (New York: Macmillan 1941), 147-8; and North China *Herald*, 9 June 1923.

24. North China *Herald*, 2 June 1923.

25. China *Weekly Review*, June 1923.

26. China *Weekly Review*, Powell's letter of 17 May 1923.

27. North China *Herald*, 2 June 1923.

28. Powell, "Golden Eggs," 956.

29. North China *Herald*, 2 June 1923.

30. Powell, "Golden Eggs," 956.

31. RG 59, 393.1123, Asiatic News Agency.

32. Peking & Tientsin *Times*, 30 May 1923.

33. RG 59, 393.1123, news clippings.

34. North China *Herald*, 9 June 1923.

35. North China *Herald*, 2 June 1923.

36. Ibid.

37. Probable participants: General Chen Tian-yuan of Kiangsu; General Hung [or Huang, chief of staff of Deputy tuchon]. Bandit chiefs evidently Sun Mei-yao, Kwei Chi-tsai [perhaps another name for Kuo]. Bo-bo Liu, probably Liu Wo-kang, and Chi Chui-chiang.

38. North China *Herald*, 9 June 1923.

39. Ibid.

40. Macleay to Curzon, 10 June 1923, FO 371/9191.

CHAPTER ELEVEN

1. Hughes to Schurman, 1 June 1923, *Foreign Relations*, 650.

2. Ibid., 651.

3. Ibid.

4. North China *Herald*, 9 June 1923.

5. Schurman to Hughes, 21 June 1923, RG 59, 393.1123/211.

6. North China *Herald*, 9 June 1923.

7. Schurman to Hughes, 21 June 1923, RG 59, 393.1123/211; & FO 371/9191.

8. Chen Wu-wo, *True Facts*, 26.

9. North China *Herald*, 9 June 1923.

10. Schurman to Hughes, 21 June 1923, RG 59, 393.1123/211.

11. Ibid.

12. Macleay to Curzon, 3 June 1923, FO 9189.

13. North China *Herald*, 9 June 1923.

14. North China *Herald*, 16 June 1923.

15. Ibid.

16. Woodhead, *The China Year Book, 1924-1925*, 1184.

17. North China *Herald*, 16 June 1923.

18. *Hansard Parliamentary Debates* (Series 5), vol 164, 2154-55.

19. Schurman to Hughes, 21 June 1923, RG 59, 393.1123/211.

20. North China *Herald*, 16 June 1923.

226 *Outrage at Lincheng*

21. Powell, China *Weekly Review*, April-May 1939.

22. Woodhead, *China Year Book, 1924-1925*, 1184.

23. Ibid.

24. Schurman to Hughes, 9 June 1923, *Foreign Relations*, 509-510.

25. Woodhead, *China Year Book, 1924-1925*, 1184.

26. Schurman to Hughes, 9 June 1923, *Foreign Relations*, 510.

27. Schurman to Hughes, 10 June 1923, *Foreign Relations*, 655.

28. North China *Herald*, 16 June 1923.

29. *Hansard*, vol 165, 15.

30. Woodhead, *China Year Book, 1924-1925*, 1184.

31. Powell, China *Weekly Review*, April-May 1939.

32. Ibid., June 1923.

33. Ibid., April-May 1939.

34. Ibid., June 1923.

35. Ibid.

36. Woodhead, *China Year Book, 1924-1925*, 1184.

37. Ibid., 1185.

38. North China *Herald*, 16 June 1923.

39. Ibid.

40. Chen Wu-wo, *True Facts*, 27.

41. Schurman to Hughes, 14 June 1923, *Foreign Relations*, 657.

CHAPTER TWELVE

1. Schurman to Hughes, 14 June 1923, *Foreign Relations,* 510.

2. *Hansard,* vol 165, 491.

3. Schurman to Hughes, 17 June 1923, *Foreign Relations,* 658.

4. Schurman to Hughes, 14 June 1923, RG 59, 393.1123/156.

5. Schurman to Hughes, 15 June 1923, *Foreign Relations,* 660.

6. Ibid.

7. Schurman to Hughes, 22 June 1923, RG 59 393.1123/167.

8. Henley to Huston, 21 June 1923, RG 59, 393.1123.

9. Schurman to Hughes, 19 June 1923, *Foreign Relations,* 661.

10. Ibid.

11. Schurman to Hughes, 20 June 1923, *Foreign Relations,* 662.

12. Schurman to Hughes, 22 June 1923, *Foreign Relations,* 664.

13. Schurman to Hughes, 20 June 1923, *Foreign Relations,* 663.

14. Hughes to Schurman, 23 June 1923, *Foreign Relations,* 667.

15. Woodhead, *China Year Book, 1924-1925,* 1185.

16. Chilton to Hughes, 30 June 1923, *Foreign Relations,* 673.

17. North China *Herald*, 7 July 1923.

18. Chan Lau Kit-ching, "The Lincheng Incident—a Case Study of British Policy in China Between the Washington Conference (1921-1922) and the First Nationalist Revolution (1925-1928), *Journal of Oriental Studies,* 10, No. 2 (1972), 179.

19. Hughes to Chilton, 9 July 1923, *Foreign Relations,* 676.

20. *China Review,* June 1923.

21. Woodhead, *China Year Book, 1924-1925,* 1185-6.

22. Chen Wu-wo, *True Facts,* 2.

23. North China *Herald,* 25 August 1923.

24. Chilton to Hughes, 30 June 1923, *Foreign Relations,* 672.

25. Schurman to Hughes, 21 August 1923, *Foreign Relations,* 689.

26. North China *Herald,* 25 August 1923.

27. Schurman to Hughes, 21 August 1923, *Foreign Relations,* 689.

28. Ibid., 690.

29. Stremski, *Britain's China Policy,* 65.

30. Schurman to Hughes, 21 August 1923, *Foreign Relations,* 689.

31. Schram, *Mao Tse-Tung,* 73.

32. DeAngelis, *Schurman,* 245.

33. Woodhead, *China Year Book 1924-1925,* 1186.

34. DeAngelis, *Schurman,* 246.

35. Koo to Schurman, 24 September 1923, *Foreign Relations,* 696.

36. Ibid.

37. North China *Herald*, 10 May 1924.

38. Schurman to Hughes, 28 September 1923, *Foreign Relations*, 694.

39. Schurman to Hughes, 5 October 1923, *Foreign Relations*, 704-5.

40. Schurman to Hughes, 5 October 1923, *Foreign Relations*, 517.

41. Schurman to Hughes, 11 October 1923, *Foreign Relations*, 518.

42. Koo to De Freitas, 15 October 1923, *Foreign Relations*, 707.

43. DeAngelis, *Schurman*, 249.

44. Chan Lau Kit-ching, "The Lincheng Incident," 186.

45. Aldrich, "A Week-End With Chinese Bandits" (November 1923), 672.

46. Tenney to Schurman, 22 December 1923, RG 59, 393.1123/278.

47. Car Crow, *The Chinese Are Like That* (New York: World Publishing Co. 1943), 324.

48. Tenney to Schurman, 22 December 1923, RG 59, 393.1123/278.

49. Chu Pao-chin, *V. K. Wellington Koo*, 208.

50. Powell, *My 25 Years In China*, 123.

51. DeAngelis, *Schurman*, 249.

52. Fairbank, *China's Response to the West*, 231-232.

53. Woodhead, *China Year Book, 1924-1925*, 829.
54. *Foreign Relations*, 709.
55. Powell, *My 25 Years In China*, 93.
56. *The China Press*, 8 May 1923.

Select Bibliography

Aldrich, Lucy T. "A Week-End With Chinese Bandits." *The Atlantic Monthly* (November 1923), 672-686.

Booker, Edna Lee. *News Is My Job.* New York: Macmillan, 1941.

Chan Lau Kit-Ching. "The Lincheng Incident—a Case Study of British Policy in China Between the Washington Conference (1921-1922) and the First Nationalist Revolution (1925-1928)." *Journal of Oriental Studies,* Hong Kong, 10 (2) (1972), 172-186.

Chen Wu-Wo. "True Facts About the Lincheng Incident." Peking: Peking Express Press, 1923. This rare bilingual Chinese and English pamphlet is very much pro Governor Tien.

Ch'i Hsi-Sheng. *Warlord Politics in China 1916-1928.* Stanford University Press, 1976.

China Review. China Trade Bureau (New York) (June 1923).

China Weekly Review (Shanghai) (May 1923-December 1923). This was J. B. Powell's journal and various of his letters from captivity were published here. Also see April 15 - May 13, 1939, for a special anniversary retrospective.

232 Select Bibliography

Crow, Carl. *The Chinese Are Like That*. New York: World Publishing Co., 1943. See pages 313-328. Although Crow wrote several books, he does not seem to have again commented on the Lincheng outrage.

Chu Pao-Chin. *V. K. Wellington Koo: A Study of the Diplomat and Diplomacy of Warlord China, During His Early Career, 1919-1924*. University of Pennsylvania, Ph.D., 1970. Ann Arbor: University Microfilms. Later published in Hong Kong.

Current History Magazine. "China, Ill-Governed and Bankrupt, Yet Prosperous" (May 1923), 320-326. "Bandits A Growing Menace In China" (July 1923), 606-610. "Shantung and its Foreign Rulers" (July 1923), 611-614.

DeAngelis, Richard Clarke. *Jacob Gould Schurman and American Policy Toward China, 1921-1925*. St. John's University, Ph.D. Ann Arbor: University Microfilms, 1975.

Far Eastern Review (New York). "After Lincheng, What?" (June 1923), 363-365.

Foreign Relations of the U.S. 1923. Vol. 1, United States Printing Office (Washington 1938), 507-524, 631-709.

Hansard Parliamentary Debates (Series 5) Volumes 162, 164-167.

Illustrated London News (23 June 1923), 1003; and (4 August 1923), 214-5.

Literary Digest (19 May 1923).

London Times (May and June 1923).

Manchester Guardian (May and June 1923).

Musso, Guiseppe D. *La Cina Ed I Cinesi, Loro Legge E Costumi*. Milano: U. Hoepli, 1926.

New York Times (May and June 1923). See *N. Y. T. Index* Vol VII.

North China Herald and *Supreme Court and Consular Gazette* (Shanghai) (May 1923-May 1924). The weekly issues of May and June 1923, published a supplement of *Lincheng News*. While occasionally inaccurate, these supplements helped with the chronology. See May 1924 for an anniversary commentary.

Peking Who's Who. Peking: Tientsin Press Ltd., 1922.

Powell, John B. *My Twenty Five Years in China*. New York: Macmillan, 1945. See pages 92-124 for an interesting overview. This volume is cited in some scholarly studies and was the catalyst for my efforts. See the *Dictionary of American Biography*, Supplement 4, 1946-1950.

_____. " 'Esteemed Guests' Of The Chinese Bandits," *ASIA* (New York), Nevember 1923, 845-848.

_____. "The Bandits' 'Golden Eggs' Depart" *ASIA* (December 1923), 914-916. Also see *China Weekly Review* above.

Public Record Office (The British), Documents from FO 371.

The Living Age. "Blue Trains and Bandits" (Autumn 1923), 450-453.

Trans-Pacific (Tokyo). "Prisoner of Chinese Bandits Describes Life in Captivity." (June 9, 1923). The *Trans-Pacific* is valuable because it reprinted various articles from tiny treatyport publications that have otherwise vanished. See May-October 1923.

United States Department of State. Decimal Files, Record Group 59, Washington D. C. 393.1123 Lincheng (Lincheng Train Kidnapping Case). Decimal file 893.105 describing the activities of the Chinese police was also useful.

The China Weekly Review. Shanghai, "Who's Who In China," 3rd ed (1926).

Woodhead, H. G. W., Ed. *The China Year Book 1924-1925*. Tientsin: The Tientsin Press Ltd. See pages 818-827 and 1178-1191.

General Bibliography

Alco Power Inc. *The Alco Story* (From 1837 Into the Future). Auburn, New York: ca. 1980.

Anderson, Flavia. *The Rebel Emperor*. New York: Doubleday, 1959.

Austin, Anthony & Robert Clurman. *The China Watchers*. Pyramid Books.

Avery, Al. *A Yankee Flier in the Far East*. New York: Grosset & Dunlap, 1942.

Backhouse, E. & J. O. P. Bland. *Annals and Memoirs of the Court of Peking*. London: William Heinemann, 1914.

Balazs, Etienne. *Chinese Civilization and Bureaucracy*. Yale University Press, 1964.

Beau, Georges, *Chinese Medicine*. New York: Avon.

Bloodsworth, Dennis. *The Chinese Looking Glass*. New York: Farrar, Straus & Giroux, 1966.

Bodde, Derk. *China's Cultural Tradition.* New York: Holt, Rinehart & Winston, 1965.

Bonosky, Phillip. *Dragon Pink On Old White.* Marzani & Munsell, 1963.

Brule, Jean-Pierre. *China Comes of Age.* Baltimore: Pelican, 1969.

Buck, Pearl. *Dragon Seed.* New York: John Day Co., 1941.

_____. *The Good Earth.* Pocket Books.

_____. *China Flight.* Blakiston—Triangle Books, 1943.

_____. *Imperial Woman.* New York: John Day Co., 1956.

Buss, Claude A. *The People's Republic of China.* Princeton: Van Nostrand, 1962.

Carr, E. H. *The Bolshevik Revolution,* Vol. III. Baltimore: Pelican, 1966.

Chang, Perry P. *China, Development By Force.* Curriculum Resources, 1964.

Chih Hsu, Mongton. *Railway Problems in China.* New York: AMS Press.

Chun, T'ien. *Village In August.* New York: World Publishing, 1944.

Clark, Gerald. *Impatient Giant: Red China Today.* New York: David McKay Co.

Clavell, James. *Tai-Pan.* New York: Dell, 1966.

Committee of Concerned Asian Scholars. *China, Inside The People's Republic.* New York: Bantam, 1972.

Coye, Molly J. & Jon Livingston. *China Yesterday & Today.* New York: Bantam, 1975.

Crozier, Brian. *South-East Asia In Turmoil.* Penguin, 1965.

Deacon, Richard. *The Chinese Secret Service.* New York: Ballantine Books, 1974.

Der Ling. *Two Years In The Forbidden City.* New York: Dodd, Mead, 1924.

Dhiegh, Khigh Alx. *I Ching.* New York: Ballantine Books, 1974.

Egerton, T. Clement. *The Golden Lotus.* London: Routledge & Kegan Paul.

Fairbank, John K. & Ssu-Yu Teng. *China's Response to the West.* New York: Atheneum, 1969.

Fairbank, John K., Edwin O. Reischauer, & Albert M. Craig. *East Asia the Modern Transformation.* Boston: Houghton Mifflin, 1965.

Fitzgerald, C. P. *The Birth of Communist China.* Baltimore: Pelican, 1966.

Galbraith, John Kenneth. *A China Passage.* Boston: Houghton Mifflin, 1973.

Gilman, Laselle. *The Dragon's Mouth.* Wm. Sloane Associates, 1954.

Goodrich, L. Carrington. *A Short History of the Chinese People.* New York: Harper and Brothers, 1943.

Gunther, John. *Inside Asia.* New York: Harper & Brothers, 1939.

Hahn, Emily. *China To Me.* New York: Garden City, 1946.

Han Suyin. *The Morning Deluge.* Great Britain: Panther, 1976.

_____. *The Crippled Tree.* Great Britain: Panther, 1965.

_____. *A Mortal Flower.* Great Britain: Panther, 1966.

_____. *Birdless Summer.* Great Britain: Panther, 1968.

238 General Bibliography

Harris, Nigel. *The Mandate of Heaven.* Quartet Books, 1978.

Hellerman, Leon & Alan L. Stein, Eds. *China: Readings on the Middle Kingdom.* New York: Washington Square Press, 1971.

Hsieh, Alice L. *Communist China's Strategy in the Nuclear Era.* A Spectrum Book.

Hunter, Guy. *South-East Asia, Race, Culture & Nation.* London: Oxford University Press, 1966.

Hutchinson, Paul. *China's Real Revolution.* New York: National Council, Department of Missions, 1924.

I Ching, A Philosophical Prophecy. New York: Reiss Games, 1972.

Jackson, W. A. Douglas. *Russo-Chinese Borderlands.* Princeton: Van Nostrand.

Lamb, Harold. *Genghis Khan.* New York: Garden City, 1927.

Lao Tzu. *Tao-Teh King.* New York: Unger, 1967.

———. *The Way Of Life.* New York: Mentor, 1955.

Leasor, James. *Mandarin Gold.* New York: Dell, 1973.

Lee, C. Y. *The Flower Drum Song.* New York: Dell.

Lin Yutang. *The Importance of Living.* New York: John Day, 1937.

Lord, Bette Bao. *Spring Moon.* New York: Avon, 1981.

Lynch, Charles. *China, One Fourth of the World.* Toronto: McCelland & Stewart, 1965.

Malraux, Andre. *Man's Fate.* New York: Vintage.

Mao Tse-tung. *Four Essays On Philosophy.* Foreign Language Press, Peking, 1968.

———. *Quotations From Chairman Mao Tse-Tung.* New York: Bantam, 1967.

General Bibliography 239

Mason, Richard. *The World of Susie Wong.* London: Collins, 1957.

McCormick, Thomas J. *China Market 1890-1901.* Chicago: Quandrangle.

Page, Martin. *The Lost Pleasures of the Great Trains.* New York: William Morrow, 1975.

Pollock, John C. *A Foreign Devil In China.* Minneapolis: World Wide Publications, 1971.

Reps, Paul. *Zen Flesh, Zen Bones.* New York: Doubleday.

Schram, Stuart. *Mao Tse-Tung.* Middlesex: Pelican, 1966.

Scidmore, E. R. *China the Long Lived Empire.* New York: The Century Co., 1900.

Scott, Munroe. *McClure, The China Years.* Penguin Books, Canada, 1979.

Shaw, Lau. *Rickshaw Boy.* Reynal & Hitchcock, 1945.

Sheridan, James. *Chinese Warlord.* Stanford University Press, 1966.

Smith, Bradley & Wan-go Weng. *China, A History In Art.* New York: Doubleday.

Stoddard. *John L. Stoddard's Lectures, China & Japan.* Chicago: Shuman, 1897.

Snow, Edgar. *Red Star Over China.* New York: Bantam, 1979.

Stremski, Richard. *Britain's China Policy 1920-1928.* University of Wisconsin, Ph.D. Ann Arbor: University Microfilms, 1968.

Sun Tzu. *The Art of War.* London: Oxford University Press, 1963.

Thomson, John. *China and Its People in Early Photographs.* New York: Dover, 1982.

Tietjen, Eunice. *China.* Chicago: Wheeler Publishing, 1935.

Tuchman, Barbara. *Stilwell and the American Experience in China.* New York: Bantam, 1970.

Waley, Arthur. *Translations From the Chinese.* New York: Vintage, 1971.

Waltham, Clea. *Chang Tzu, Genius of the Absurd.* Ace, 1971.

Ward, Barbara. *The Interplay of East and West.* New York: Norton, 1957.

Watts, Allen W. *The Way of Zen.* New York: Pantheon, 1957.

White, Theodore H. *China, the Roots of Madness.* New York: Bantam, 1969.

Wou, Odoric Ying-kwong. *Militarism In Modern China: The Career of Wu Pei-fu, 1916-1939.* Ph.D. Studies of the East Asian Institute, Columbia University. Ann Arbor: University Microfilms, 1978. Later published in Australia.

Wu, John C. H. *Beyond East and West.* London: Sheed & Ward, 1952.

INDEX

Aldrich, Lucy T., 2-5, 8-13, 55, 72, 134-136, 182-183
Allen, Martha, 5, 13, 17-18
Allen, Major Robert, 5, 37, 39, 54, 60, 67, 111, 122, 124, 140-141, 143, 172
American Car & Foundry, 101
American Locomotive Co., 101
Anderson, Roy S., 42, 76, 78, 80, 110-111, 113, 125, 137-138, 140-142, 147, 151, 155-162
Annam, 27, 84, 94

Berube, Marcel, 3, 38, 60-61, 66, 79, 115, 117-118, 125
Booker, Edna Lee, 134-135
Boxer Rebellion, 28-29, 74, 96, 136, 158, 169

Chang Chin-yao, 47, 51, 110
Chang Hsun, 47, 100, 109
Chang Shao-tseng, 73, 131, 152-153
Chang Tso-lin, 32, 47, 101, 105, 109
Chiang Kai-shek, 177
Coltman, Charles, 32-33
Confucius, 32, 39, 81-82, 93, 102, 137
Conner, William, 147, 156

Coralti, Alba, 9-10, 71-72
Crow, Carl, 42, 78, 123

Davis, John K., 75, 78-80, 138, 150
Day, Thomas, 2-3, 7, 19, 72
De Freitas, J. Bathalha, 72-73, 182

Elias, Eddie, 38-39, 147, 149
Elias, Fred, 39, 54, 59, 149, 165

Feng, Yu-hsiang, 137, 150, 153, 159
France, 19, 22, 25-29, 47-48, 50, 72, 94-95, 100, 103, 107-108, 128, 144, 147, 150, 165, 169, 171, 175
Friedman, Leon, 37-39, 42, 59-60, 62, 111, 121-122, 132, 154, 165-166

Gensburger, Emile, 38, 165
Germany, 17, 28-30, 48, 50, 95, 98, 100, 103, 123
Gilbert, Rodney, 128, 151
Gladstone, William, 25

Haimovitch, Victor, 4, 15
Harding, Warren G., 31, 131, 145, 175
Heinze, Carl, 2, 15

242 Index

Henley, Jerome, 38, 43, 110-111, 146, 149, 151, 170
Ho Chi minh, 30
Ho Feng-yu, 42, 52, 74, 108-109, 112, 147, 171
Holbrook, Sir A., 168-169
Hughes, Charles Evans, 31, 131, 145, 172, 174
Hung, Dr. Siji C., 38, 60, 127, 159, 164
Hutchinson, Paul, 2, 103-104

Italy, 19, 21, 26, 28-29, 72, 75, 83, 95, 103, 107-108, 150, 165, 171

Jacobsen, M.C., 2, 7-8, 19, 46, 72
Japan, 21, 27-31, 48, 51, 53, 75, 85, 95, 98, 100, 102, 106, 108-109, 147, 165, 169-171, 173-178
Jesuits, 21-23, 86-87

Kang Tung-yi, 18
King George III, 23-24, 88-90
Koo, Dr. V.K. Wellington, 33, 118, 153, 155-156, 175-182
Korea, 27-28, 94, 97
Kuomintang, 47, 98, 177

League of Nations, 102
Lehrbas, Lloyd, 3, 5, 13-18, 185
Lenfers, William, 17, 39-40, 54, 112-113, 142
Li Yuan-hung, 33, 97, 105-106, 125, 131, 150, 153-155, 157, 159, 165, 168, 171, 174, 178
Lin Tse-hsu, 24, 91-92

Macleay, Sir Ronald, 72, 74, 76, 130, 143, 151, 169-170, 175-176
Mao, Tse-tung, 51-footnote #9, 177
May 4th Movement, 30, 100
McFadden, Minnie, 2-4, 19, 36, 71-72
Mertons, Dr. Paul, 54-55, 62-65, 112
Milbourne, Harvey L., 18, 70-72, 74-75

Musso, Guiseppe D., 7, 9, 37-38, 40, 43, 54, 59, 62, 111-112, 121, 132, 142, 145, 150-151, 154, 165-166

Naill, 12-13, 18, 70-71, 73-75, 106-109, 134, 136
Nestorians, 21, 83

Opium, 23-27, 38, 51, 61, 68, 85, 90-92, 153, 160
Orpen-Palmer, H.B., 147

Philoon, Wallace, 47, 78-80
Pinger, Miriam, 3, 4, 13, 18
Pinger, Roland, 3, 4, 36, 38, 60, 67, 73, 111, 120, 122, 124, 131, 141, 165, 170, 172
Polo, Marco, 2, 21, 83
Pope Pius XI, 142
Portugal, 21-23, 72, 84-86
Potte, August, 145, 154
Powell, John B., 3, 6-7, 13, 18, 35, 37-38, 48-49, 57, 59, 61, 63-64, 71, 111, 122, 127, 131-132, 137-140, 150, 154, 159, 165-166, 185
Pu Yi, 97, 100

Queen Victoria, 24, 92, 97

Ricci, Matteo, 85-86
Rockefeller, John D., 13, 55
Rothman, Joseph, 18, 70-71
Rowlatt, Reginal, 2-3, 38, 57, 60, 65, 76, 122, 147, 149, 165
Russia, 26, 28-29, 47-48, 87, 95, 101, 177

Saphiere, Theo, 38, 59, 148
Schurman, Dr. Jacob Gould, 18-19, 31, 33-34, 70-71, 78-80, 125, 128, 131, 145, 151, 153, 155-156, 167, 170, 172, 177, 181, 183
Shanghai-Wusung Railroad, 27, 93-94
Smith, Arthur H., 20-21

Index 243

Smith, William, 4-5, 38, 59, 126, 130, 141-142
Solomon, Lee, 38, 59-60, 67, 122, 124, 131, 140-141, 143, 154, 159, 163-165
Sun Yat-sen, 97-98, 100, 106, 109, 174, 177, 181

Tien Chung-yu, 106-110, 112, 118, 125, 128, 131-132, 139, 171, 178, 181-182, 184
Tientsin-Pukow Railway, 29, 42, 53, 74, 76, 101, 110, 125, 145, 169
Tours, B.G., 150
Treaty of Versailles, 30, 100-101
Tsao Kun, 72, 79, 101, 106, 108-109, 116, 131, 151, 154-156, 173-174, 180-181
Tsu Hsi, 94-97

Verea, Manuel & Sra., 7, 37-38, 54, 59-60, 67-68, 80, 132, 147, 149
Vietnam, 27, 95 (see Annam)
Voltaire, 20

Wainwright, J. M., 151
Washington Conference, 31-32, 102-103
Wen, Shih-chen (S.T. Wen), 76, 78, 108, 110-111, 113, 140, 148, 151, 160, 161
Whitham, Paul P., 17, 70
Wilson, Woodrow, 30, 100
World War I (Great War), 30, 50, 76, 98-99, 101-102
Wu Chang-chi, 19, 74, 106, 147-148
Wu Pei-fu, 101, 173
Wu Yu-lin, 108, 112, 115, 117, 118, 128

Yang-I-teh, 108, 112, 115, 117, 118
Yen, Dr. W.W., 153, 155
Yerks, Carroll, 41
Yuan Shih-k'ai, 95, 97-99

Zimmerman, A.L., 2, 4, 6, 15